THE FOLGER LIBRARY SHAKESPEARE

Designed to make Shakespeare's classic plays available to the general reader, each edition contains a reliable text with modernized spelling and punctuation, scene-by-scene plot summaries, and explanatory notes clarifying obscure and obsolete expressions. An interpretive essay and accounts of Shakespeare's life and theater form an instructive preface to each play.

Louis B. Wright, General Editor, was the Director of the Folger Shakespeare Library from 1948 until his retirement in 1968. He is the author of *Middle-Class Culture in Elizabethan England, Religion and Empire, Shakespeare for Everyman,* and many other books and essays on the history and literature of the Tudor and Stuart periods.

Virginia Lamar, Assistant Editor, served as research assistant to the Director and Executive Secretary of the Folger Shakespeare Library from 1946 until her death in 1968. She is the author of *English Dress in the Age of Shakespeare* and *Travel and Roads in England,* and coeditor of William Strachey's *Historie of Travell into Virginia Britania.*

The Folger Shakespeare Library

THE
TAMING OF
THE SHREW

by

WILLIAM
SHAKESPEARE

WASHINGTON SQUARE PRESS
PUBLISHED BY POCKET BOOKS NEW YORK

A Washington Square Press Publication of
POCKET BOOKS, a Simon & Schuster division of
GULF & WESTERN CORPORATION
1230 Avenue of the Americas, New York, N.Y. 10020

ISBN: 0-671-43687-2

First Pocket Books printing April, 1963

30   29   28   27   26   25   24

WASHINGTON SQUARE PRESS WSP and colophon are trademarks
of Simon & Schuster.

Printed in the U.S.A.

Preface

This edition of *The Taming of the Shrew* is designed to make available a readable text of one of Shakespeare's early comedies. In the centuries since Shakespeare, many changes have occurred in the meanings of words, and some clarification of Shakespeare's vocabulary may be helpful. To provide the reader with necessary notes in the most accessible format, we have placed them on the pages facing the text that they explain. We have tried to make these notes as brief and simple as possible. Preliminary to the text we have also included a brief statement of essential information about Shakespeare and his stage. Readers desiring more detailed information should refer to the books suggested in the references, and if still further information is needed, the bibliographies in those books will provide the necessary clues to the literature of the subject.

The early texts of Shakespeare's plays provide only scattered stage directions and no indications of setting, and it is conventional for modern editors to add these to clarify the action. Such additions, and additions to entrances and exits, as well as many indications of act and scene division, are placed in square brackets.

All illustrations are from material in the Folger Library collections.

L. B. W.

V. A. L.

September 1, 1962

War of the Sexes

Sentimental critics of the Victorian period and sociologically minded critics of the twentieth century have been inclined to apologize for Shakespeare's attitude toward women as revealed in *The Taming of the Shrew*. They have noted that Petruchio's treatment of Katherina is harsh and brutal, not at all the sort of behavior that one might expect of a proper English gentleman, even though Shakespeare did translate his hero to Italy and make him a citizen of Verona. Protagonists of women's rights have taken Shakespeare to task for his cavalier disregard of elementary justice to women and his own apparent approval of Petruchio's conduct. John Masefield, writing in 1911, called the language that Shakespeare puts into the mouth of the broken Katherina "melancholy claptrap" and sadly described Petruchio as "a boor who cares only for his own will, her flesh, and her money." In short, the poet laureate thinks Shakespeare is not at his romantic best in this play. Later, in 1929, John Bailey asserted that *The Taming of the Shrew* was a blot on the fair record of English civilization: "It is rather strange that the play is still acted, for it is, to tell the truth, an ugly and barbarous as well as a very confused, prosaic, and tedious affair." And quoting a German scholar who noted that the play was popular in Germany because the Germans loved practical jokes, Bailey added: "No play exhibits more of this obsolete form of amusement than *The Taming of the Shrew*, and the fact that it still appears on the stage goes some way to deprive us of the credit for civilization which this generous German was ready to give us."

Despite the overrefined tastes reflected in these comments, *The Taming of the Shrew* has been persistently popular since Shakespeare's day, for it is a boisterous and amusing farce on a theme that has entertained both men and women since the beginning of time: the conflict between the sexes and the comic situations that this eternal warfare begets. Shakespeare was not writing a treatise on sociology; he was not even putting on the stage the doctrines laid down in numerous contemporary handbooks on behavior. He was writing a stage success—he hoped —and he made the situations as comic as possible, even at the expense of offending a later poet laureate of proper Englishmen.

The Taming of the Shrew has puzzled and vexed Shakespearean scholars on other grounds, for they cannot agree about its relation to another play with a similar name, *The Taming of a Shrew*, which was printed in 1594 with a statement on the title page that "it was sundry times acted by the Right Honorable the Earl of Pembroke his servants." Some argue

that the printed version of *A Shrew* was a corrupt
quarto reproduced from *The Shrew* memorially,
that is, by one or more actors who knew the parts.
Sir Edmund Chambers and most other recent scholars reject this view and regard *A Shrew* as the older
play, which Shakespeare—and perhaps a collaborator—reworked into *The Shrew* as we know it. Chambers holds that *The Shrew* shows evidence of another hand besides Shakespeare's, particularly in the
subplot concerning Bianca and her suitors. Although
some passages in the Bianca scenes, it is true, are
not in Shakespeare's characteristic vein, no decisive
proof exists that he had a collaborator in reworking
an old farce into a play that shows evidence of having been hurriedly put together. Shakespeare himself was not above hasty work on occasion, and
while he may have had a collaborator, the presence
of pedestrian passages in the play does not consti-
tute convincing evidence of the handiwork of a
lesser writer.

Others have advanced somewhat different expla-
nations of the relations between *A Shrew* and *The
Shrew*. One is that an early and now lost *Shrew* play
by Shakespeare was reconstructed by actors into *A
Shrew* and that *The Shrew* as we now have it repre-
sents a reworking by Shakespeare of his own early
version. After surveying all the scholarship on the
subject, John Munro in *The London Shakespeare*
concludes: "A reasonable explanation of the relation of *A Shrew* and *The Shrew* which seems to fit
the evidence is that *A Shrew* is the actors' reported
version of the source-play of *The Shrew* into which

has been transferred a good deal of Shakespeare's text, with some distortion."

The fact that two *Shrew* plays by different companies could hold the stage is indicative of the Elizabethans' liking for the theme. By Shakespeare's time the farcical battle of the sexes already had a long history in both fiction and drama. Many folk tales, some of which were crystallized in Chaucer, made use of the age-old combat between husbands and wives, with sometimes the husband victor, sometimes the wife. Long before Shakespeare, in the biblical play on the Flood, Noah provided audiences with a vast amount of enjoyment by beating his wife "black and blue" because she refused to go into the ark. Nobody thought to complain about this example of cruelty to women in an age when the common law prescribed that a man might beat a froward and stubborn wife with a stick, provided it was no bigger than his thumb. In the interludes of John Heywood performed during the reign of Henry VIII, the ancient battle of the sexes was a dominant theme. Numerous Tudor and Stuart plays, before and after Shakespeare, continued to find this topic fresh and entertaining. John Fletcher wrote a kind of rebuttal to Shakespeare's *Shrew* in *The Woman's Prize; or, The Tamer Tamed* (ca. 1604), in which the man gets the worst of the conflict. Over and over again this topic finds its way into drama, and it is one of the most persistent of all dramatic themes, as old as Adam and as modern as Noel Coward.

Audiences and readers—except those serious souls

who must see a profound lesson in all literature—have enjoyed *The Taming of the Shrew* for what it is, an entertaining farce on a topic of eternal interest. Shakespeare knew precisely what he was doing when he prepared the comedy for the stage. He expected his audience to accept the conventions for this kind of comedy and to disregard absurdities of plot and even of characterization. He was not writing a realistic comedy of manners but was breathing new life into a set of stock situations that audiences had found laughable since the beginning of comic drama.

Even though *The Taming of the Shrew* is essentially a farce, it is a cut above most farcical comedy of its day and is a great improvement on *A Shrew,* which is cruder and has more horseplay than Shakespeare's version. Shakespeare does not have Petruchio gain his comic effects by the coarse methods beloved of the groundlings—by showing Petruchio actually beating his wife, as did the husband in the earlier Noah play, for example, and in some crude Elizabethan comedies. On the contrary, Petruchio pretends to be concerned only for Katherina's welfare. He will not let her eat a morsel of burned meat, which might make her choleric; he will not permit her to wear a custard-coffin of a cap, which, he asserts, is not good enough for her. Everything that he does to tame her, he does with excessive claims of his great love. In the end, Katherina is really in love with her lord and master, and her speech to the "froward wives" on the duty of obedience has the ring of sincerity. Petruchio has not only tamed her; he has won her and converted her disposition. In this transformation Shakespeare goes beyond ordinary farce and achieves genuine comedy.

The Taming of the Shrew begins with the dramatic device of a framework to make the comedy a play within a play. The Induction, in which drunken Christopher Sly is made to believe that he is a noble lord witnessing a play in his great hall, provides the framework, which Shakespeare took from his source. But after the first scene of Act I, Shakespeare abandons the framework and Sly, whereas in his source Sly is retained until the end. The Induction provides an opportunity for Shakespeare to insert some atmosphere from his native Warwickshire. The description of the hunting scene, the names of the dogs, the name of Sly himself (suggested perhaps by Stephen Sly, a man of Stratford), place names like Burton Heath (for Barton-on-the-Heath) and Greece (for Greet not far from Winchcomb), the reference to Marian Hacket, "the fat alewife of Wincot" (where Shakespeare himself had doubtless drunk its famous ale)—all of these allusions give a sense of reality to the opening of the play and reflect the delight in an English setting characteristic of Shakespeare whether the nominal locale of his play is Italy, France, Rome, or Egypt. Even if the source play had a more elaborate Induction, Shakespeare transformed his framework into something that revealed his own background—like the signature of a painter tucked into the corner of a canvas.

Without much doubt, Shakespeare merely reworked an old play that was his immediate source, but the ultimate sources of the plot and situations are various. The practical joke on Sly has numerous literary parallels, including an incident related by Marco Polo. The subduing of a shrewish wife is one of the commonest themes in folk literature. The Bianca episodes are similar to situations in Ariosto's play *I Suppositi*, which George Gascoigne translated as *The Supposes* (1566).

DATE, HISTORY, AND TEXT

The determination of the date of the first performance of *The Taming of the Shrew* depends upon its relation to *A Shrew*, printed in 1594 and acted sometime before that by the Earl of Pembroke's Men. Chambers thinks that *The Shrew* probably was composed in some haste in 1593 or early 1594 and acted soon thereafter. A performance in 1593-1594, which is consonant with the evidence, places this play in the early group of Shakespeare's plays, the only ones preceding it being the three parts of *Henry VI*, *Richard III*, *The Comedy of Errors*, and *Titus Andronicus*.

No quarto version of *The Taming of the Shrew* was printed before its inclusion in the First Folio in 1623, but a quarto edition, printed from the Folio text, was brought out in 1631. The title page described the comedy as "acted by His Majesty's servants at the Blackfriars and the Globe." Although not much evidence remains for the stage history of

The Taming of the Shrew in Shakespeare's day, it apparently was a success. The fact that Fletcher chose to write a stage rebuttal in *The Woman's Prize; or, The Tamer Tamed* suggests that he was capitalizing on the popularity of Shakespeare's play. *The Shrew* had a revival at court in 1633.

After the reopening of the theatres at the Restoration of Charles II in 1660, *The Taming of the Shrew* was one of Shakespeare's plays chosen for adaptation to the new stage. An actor named John Lacy revised the comedy into something called *Sauny the Scot*, which bore little resemblance to the original. After the Jacobite rebellion of the Scots in 1715, Charles Johnson took the Induction to *The Shrew* and made it over into a political travesty entitled *The Cobbler of Preston*, which satirized the Scottish rebels. Johnson's piece was designed for Drury Lane. A rival comedian stole the title and put on a similar burlesque at Lincoln's Inn Fields. In 1635, a revision of *Sauny the Scot* called *A Cure for a Scold* appeared on the stage of Drury Lane, the handiwork of James Worsdale. Finally, in 1754, David Garrick returned to Shakespeare's original and, using the title *Catherine and Petruchio*, made a three-act adaptation of his own for performance at Drury Lane. Garrick's streamlined version, which omitted the Induction and some of the complications of the Bianca plot, was extremely popular and was frequently acted throughout the eighteenth and nineteenth centuries. It was not until 1887 that Augustin Daly first performed Shakespeare's original play in the United States. Even after that, producers continued to use Garrick's abbreviated version, and, Professor Hazelton Spencer observes, "it is still occasionally acted by misguided amateurs."

Shakespeare's comedy has been one of his most popular plays in the twentieth century. It is frequently played as even broader farce than Shakespeare intended, as, for example, the well-received production by Alfred Lunt and Lynn Fontanne. It had successful motion-picture performances and provided the basic theme for the extraordinarily popular musical show, *Kiss Me Kate*.

The text for modern editions of *The Shrew* is necessarily based on that in the First Folio, since it had no earlier printing. The copy for the First Folio text was clearly a playhouse manuscript. At one point in the Induction the name of an actor, Sincklo, who is known to have been in the employ of the Lord Chamberlain's Men, remains as one speech prefix, and other actors' names may be retained in a few other prefixes.

THE AUTHOR

As early as 1598 Shakespeare was so well known as a literary and dramatic craftsman that Francis Meres, in his *Palladis Tamia: Wits Treasury*, referred in flattering terms to him as "mellifluous and honey-tongued Shakespeare," famous for his *Venus and Adonis*, his *Lucrece*, and "his sugared sonnets," which were circulating "among his private friends." Meres observes further that "as Plautus and Seneca are accounted the best for comedy and tragedy among the Latins, so Shakespeare among the English is the most excellent in both kinds for the stage," and he mentions a dozen plays that had made a name for Shakespeare. He concludes with the remark "that the Muses would speak with Shakespeare's fine filed phrase if they would speak English."

To those acquainted with the history of the Elizabethan and Jacobean periods, it is incredible that anyone should be so naïve or ignorant as to doubt the reality of Shakespeare as the author of the plays that bear his name. Yet so much nonsense has been written about other "candidates" for the plays that it is well to remind readers that no credible evidence that would stand up in a court of law has ever been adduced to prove either that Shakespeare did not write his plays or that anyone else wrote them. All the theories offered for the authorship of Francis Bacon, the Earl of Derby, the Earl of Oxford, the Earl of Hertford, Christopher Marlowe, and a score of other candidates are mere conjectures spun from the active imaginations of persons who confuse hypothesis and conjecture with evidence.

As Meres' statement of 1598 indicates, Shakespeare was already a popular playwright whose name carried weight at the box office. The obvious reputation of Shakespeare as early as 1598 makes the effort to prove him a myth one of the most absurd in the history of human perversity.

The anti-Shakespeareans talk darkly about a plot of vested interests to maintain the authorship of Shakespeare. Nobody has any vested interest in Shakespeare, but every scholar is interested in the truth and in the quality of evidence advanced by special pleaders who set forth hypotheses in place of facts.

The anti-Shakespeareans base their arguments upon a few simple premises, all of them false. These false premises are that Shakespeare was an unlettered yokel without any schooling, that nothing is known about Shakespeare, and that only a noble lord or the equivalent in background could have written the plays. The facts are that more is known about Shakespeare than about most dramatists of his day, that he had a very good education, acquired in the Stratford Grammar School, that the plays show no evidence of profound book learning, and that the knowledge of kings and courts evident in the plays is no greater than any intelligent young man could have picked up at second hand. Most anti-Shakespeareans are naïve and betray an obvious snobbery. The author of their favorite plays, they imply, must have had a college diploma framed and hung on his study wall like the one in their dentist's office, and obviously so great a writer must have had a title or some equally significant evidence of exalted social background. They forget that genius has a way of cropping up in unexpected places and that none of the great creative writers of the world got his inspiration in a college or university course.

William Shakespeare was the son of John Shakespeare of Stratford-upon-Avon, a substantial citizen of that small but busy market town in the center of the rich agricultural county of Warwick. John Shakespeare kept a shop, what we would call a general store; he dealt in wool and other produce and gradually acquired property. As a youth, John Shakespeare had learned the trade of glover and leather worker. There is no contemporary evidence that the elder Shakespeare was a butcher, though the anti-Shakespeareans like to talk about the ignorant "butcher's boy of Stratford." Their only evidence is a statement by gossipy John Aubrey, more than a century after William Shakespeare's birth, that young William followed his father's trade, and when he killed a calf, "he would do it in a high style and make a speech." We would like to believe the story true, but Aubrey is not a very credible witness.

John Shakespeare probably continued to operate a farm at Snitterfield that his father had leased. He married Mary Arden, daughter of his father's landlord, a man of some property. The third of their eight children was William, baptized on April 26, 1564, and probably born three days before. At least, it is conventional to celebrate April 23 as his birthday.

The Stratford records give considerable information about John Shakespeare. We know that he held several municipal offices including those of alderman and mayor. In 1580 he was in some sort of legal difficulty and was fined for neglecting a summons of the Court of Queen's Bench requiring him to appear at Westminster and be bound over to keep the peace.

As a citizen and alderman of Stratford, John Shakespeare was entitled to send his son to the grammar school free. Though the records are lost, there can be no reason to doubt that this is where young William received his education. As any student of the period knows, the grammar schools provided the basic education in Latin learning and literature. The Elizabethan grammar school is not to be confused with modern grammar schools. Many cultivated men of the day received all their formal education in the grammar schools. At the universities in this period a student would have received little training that would have inspired him to be a creative writer. At Stratford young Shakespeare would have acquired a familiarity with Latin and some little knowledge of Greek. He would have read Latin authors and become acquainted with the plays of Plautus and Terence. Undoubtedly, in this period of his life he received that stimulation to read and explore for himself the world of ancient and modern history which he later utilized in his plays. The youngster who does not acquire this type of intellectual curiosity *before* college days rarely develops as a result of a college course the kind of mind Shakespeare demonstrated. His learning in books was anything but profound, but he clearly had the probing curiosity that sent him in search of information, and he had a keenness in the observation of nature and of humankind that finds reflection in his poetry.

There is little documentation for Shakespeare's boyhood. There is little reason why there should be. Nobody knew that he was going to be a dramatist about whom any scrap of information would be prized in the centuries to come. He was merely an active and vigorous youth of Stratford, perhaps assisting his father in his business, and no Boswell bothered to write down facts about him. The most important record that we have is a marriage license issued by the Bishop of Worcester on November 27, 1582, to permit William Shakespeare to marry Anne Hathaway, seven or eight years his senior; furthermore, the Bishop permitted the marriage after reading the banns only once instead of three times, evidence of the desire for haste. The need was explained on May 26, 1583, when the christening of Susanna, daughter of William and Anne Shakespeare, was recorded at Stratford. Two years later, on February 2, 1585, the records show the birth of twins to the Shakespeares, a boy and a girl who were christened Hamnet and Judith.

What William Shakespeare was doing in Stratford during the early years of his married life, or when he went to London, we do not know. It has been conjectured that he tried his hand at schoolteaching, but that is a mere guess. There is a legend that he left Stratford to escape a charge of poaching in the park of Sir Thomas Lucy of Charlecote, but there is no proof of this. There is also a legend that when first he came to London he earned his living by holding horses outside a playhouse and presently was given employment inside, but there is nothing better than eighteenth-century hearsay for this. How Shakespeare broke into the London theatres as a dramatist and actor we do not know. But lack of information is not surprising, for Elizabethans did not write their autobiographies, and we know even less about the lives of many writers and some men of affairs than we know about Shakespeare. By 1592 he was so well established and popular that he incurred the envy of the dramatist and pamphleteer Robert Greene, who referred to him as an "upstart crow . . . in his own conceit the only Shake-scene in a country." From this time onward, contemporary allusions and references in legal documents enable the scholar to chart Shakespeare's career with greater accuracy than is possible with most other Elizabethan dramatists.

By 1594 Shakespeare was a member of the company of actors known as the Lord Chamberlain's Men. After the accession of James I, in 1603, the company would have the sovereign for their patron and would be known as the King's Men. During the period of its greatest prosperity, this company would have as its principal theatres the Globe and the Blackfriars. Shakespeare was both an actor and a shareholder in the company. Tradition has assigned him such acting roles as Adam in *As You Like It* and the Ghost in *Hamlet*, a modest place on the stage that suggests that he may have had other duties in the management of the company. Such conclusions, however, are based on surmise.

What we do know is that his plays were popular and that he was highly successful in his vocation. His first play may have been *The Comedy of Errors*, acted perhaps in 1591. Certainly this was one of his earliest plays. The three parts of *Henry VI* were acted sometime between 1590 and 1592. Critics are not in agreement about precisely how much Shakespeare wrote of these three plays. *Richard III* probably dates from 1593. With this play Shakespeare captured the imagination of Elizabethan audiences, then enormously interested in historical plays. With *Richard III* Shakespeare also gave an interpretation pleasing to the Tudors of the rise to power of the grandfather of Queen Elizabeth. From this time onward, Shakespeare's plays followed on the stage in rapid succession: *Titus Andronicus, The Taming of the Shrew, The Two Gentlemen of Verona, Love's Labor's Lost, Romeo and Juliet, Richard II, A Midsummer Night's Dream, King John, The Merchant of Venice, Henry IV (Parts 1 and 2), Much Ado About Nothing, Henry V, Julius Cæsar, As You Like It, Twelfth Night, Hamlet, The Merry Wives of Windsor, All's Well That Ends Well, Measure for Measure, Othello, King Lear*, and nine others that followed before Shakespeare retired completely, about 1613.

In the course of his career in London, he made enough money to enable him to retire to Stratford with a competence. His purchase on May 4, 1597, of New Place, then the second-largest dwelling in Stratford, a "pretty house of brick and timber," with a handsome garden, indicates his increasing prosperity. There his wife and children lived while he busied himself in the London theatres. The summer before he acquired New Place, his life was darkened by the death of his only son, Hamnet, a child of eleven. In May, 1602, Shakespeare purchased one hundred and seven acres of fertile farmland near Stratford and a few months later bought a cottage and garden across the alley from New Place. About 1611, he seems to have returned permanently to Stratford, for the next year a legal document refers to him as "William Shakespeare of Stratford-upon-Avon . . . gentleman." To achieve the desired appellation of gentleman, William Shakespeare had seen to it that the College of Heralds in 1596 granted his father a coat of arms. In one step he thus became a second-generation gentleman.

Shakespeare's daughter Susanna made a good match in 1607 with Dr. John Hall, a prominent and prosperous Stratford physician. His second daughter, Judith, did not marry until she was thirty-two years old, and then, under somewhat scandalous circumstances, she married Thomas Quiney, a Stratford vintner. On March 25, 1616, Shakespeare made his will, bequeathing his landed property to Susanna, £300 to Judith, certain sums to other relatives, and his second-best bed to his wife, Anne. Much has been made of the second-best bed, but the legacy

probably indicates only that Anne liked that particular bed. Shakespeare, following the practice of the
time, may have already arranged with Susanna for
his wife's care. Finally, on April 23, 1616, the anni-
versary of his birth, William Shakespeare died, and
he was buried on April 25 within the chancel of
Trinity Church, as befitted an honored citizen. On
August 6, 1623, a few months before the publication
of the collected edition of Shakespeare's plays, Anne
Shakespeare joined her husband in death.

THE PUBLICATION OF HIS PLAYS

During his lifetime Shakespeare made no effort to
publish any of his plays, though eighteen appeared
in print in single-play editions known as quartos.
Some of these are corrupt versions known as "bad
quartos." No quarto, so far as is known, had the
author's approval. Plays were not considered "literature" any more than most radio and television
scripts today are considered literature. Dramatists
sold their plays outright to the theatrical companies
and it was usually considered in the company's interest to keep plays from getting into print. To
achieve a reputation as a man of letters, Shakespeare wrote his *Sonnets* and his narrative poems,
Venus and Adonis and *The Rape of Lucrece*, but
he probably never dreamed that his plays would
establish his reputation as a literary genius. Only
Ben Jonson, a man known for his colossal conceit,
had the crust to call his plays *Works,* as he did

when he published an edition in 1616. But men laughed at Ben Jonson.

After Shakespeare's death, two of his old colleagues in the King's Men, John Heminges and Henry Condell, decided that it would be a good thing to print, in more accurate versions than were then available, the plays already published and eighteen additional plays not previously published in quarto. In 1623 appeared *Mr. William· Shakespeares Comedies, Histories, & Tragedies. Published according to the True Originall Copies. London. Printed by Isaac Iaggard and Ed. Blount*. This was the famous First Folio, a work that had the authority of Shakespeare's associates. The only play commonly attributed to Shakespeare that was omitted in the First Folio was *Pericles*. In their preface, "To the great Variety of Readers," Heminges and Condell state that whereas "you were abused with diverse stolen and surreptitious copies, maimed and deformed by the frauds and stealths of injurious impostors that exposed them, even those are now offered to your view cured and perfect of their limbs; and all the rest, absolute in their numbers, as he conceived them." What they used for printer's copy is one of the vexed problems of scholarship, and skilled bibliographers have devoted years of study to the question of the relation of the "copy" for the First Folio to Shakespeare's manuscripts. In some cases it is clear that the editors corrected printed quarto versions of the plays, probably by comparison with playhouse scripts: Whether these scripts were in Shakespeare's autograph is anybody's guess. No manuscript of any play in Shakespeare's handwriting has survived. Indeed, very few play manuscripts from this period by any author are extant. The Tudor and Stuart periods had not yet learned to prize autographs and authors' original manuscripts.

Since the First Folio contains eighteen plays not previously printed, it is the only source for these. For the other eighteen, which had appeared in quarto versions, the First Folio also has the authority of an edition prepared and overseen by Shakespeare's colleagues and professional associates. But since editorial standards in 1623 were far from strict, and Heminges and Condell were actors rather than editors by profession, the texts are sometimes careless. The printing and proofreading of the First Folio also left much to be desired, and some garbled passages have had to be corrected and emended. The "good quarto" texts have to be taken into account in preparing a modern edition.

Because of the great popularity of Shakespeare through the centuries, the First Folio has become a prized book, but it is not a very rare one, for it is estimated that 238 copies are extant. The Folger Shakespeare Library in Washington, D.C., has seventy-nine copies of the First Folio, collected by the founder, Henry Clay Folger, who believed that a collation of as many texts as possible would reveal significant facts about the text of Shakespeare's plays. Dr. Charlton Hinman, using an ingenious machine of his own invention for mechanical collating, has made many discoveries that throw light on Shakespeare's text and on printing practices of the day.

The probability is that the First Folio of 1623 had an edition of between 1,000 and 1,250 copies. It is believed that it sold for £1, which made it an expensive book, for £1 in 1623 was equivalent to something between $40 and $50 in modern purchasing power.

During the seventeenth century, Shakespeare was sufficiently popular to warrant three later editions in folio size, the Second Folio of 1632, the Third Folio of 1663–1664, and the Fourth Folio of 1685. The Third Folio added six other plays ascribed to Shakespeare, but these are apocryphal.

THE SHAKESPEAREAN THEATRE

The theatres in which Shakespeare's plays were performed were vastly different from those we know today. The stage was a platform that jutted out into the area now occupied by the first rows of seats on the main floor, what is called the "orchestra" in America and the "pit" in England. This platform had no curtain to come down at the ends of acts and scenes. And although simple stage properties were available, the Elizabethan theatre lacked both the machinery and the elaborate movable scenery of the modern theatre. In the rear of the platform stage was a curtained area that could be used as an inner room, a tomb, or any such scene that might be required. A balcony above this inner room, and perhaps balconies on the sides of the stage, could represent the upper deck of a ship, the entry to Juliet's room, or a prison window. A trap door in the stage provided an entrance for ghosts and devils from the nether regions, and a similar trap in the canopied structure over the stage, known as the "heavens," made it possible to let down angels on a rope. These primitive stage arrangements help to account for many elements in Elizabethan plays. For example, since there was no curtain, the dramatist frequently felt the necessity of writing into his play action to clear the stage at the ends of acts and scenes. The funeral march at the end of *Hamlet* is not there merely for atmosphere; Shakespeare had to get the corpses off the stage. The lack of scenery also freed the dramatist from undue concern about the exact location of his sets, and the physical relation of his various settings to each other did not have to be worked out with the same precision as in the modern theatre.

Before London had buildings designed exclusively for theatrical entertainment, plays were given in inns and taverns. The characteristic inn of the period had an inner courtyard with rooms opening onto balconies overlooking the yard. Players could set up their temporary stages at one end of the yard and audiences could find seats on the balconies out of the weather. The poorer sort could stand or sit on the cobblestones in the yard, which was open to the sky. The first theatres followed this construction, and throughout the Elizabethan period the large public theatres had a yard in front of the stage open to the weather, with two or three tiers of covered balconies extending around the theatre. This physical structure again influenced the writing of plays. Because a dramatist wanted the actors to be heard, he frequently wrote into his play orations that could be delivered with declamatory effect. He also provided spectacle, buffoonery, and broad jests to keep the riotous groundlings in the yard entertained and quiet.

In another respect the Elizabethan theatre differed greatly from ours. It had no actresses. All women's roles were taken by boys, sometimes recruited from the boys' choirs of the London churches. Some of these youths acted their roles with great skill and the Elizabethans did not seem to be aware of any incongruity. The first actresses on the professional English stage appeared after the Restoration of Charles II, in 1660, when exiled Englishmen brought back from France practices of the French stage.

London in the Elizabethan period, as now, was the center of theatrical interest, though wandering actors from time to time traveled through the country performing in inns, halls, and the houses of the nobility. The first professional playhouse, called simply The Theatre, was erected by James Burbage, father of Shakespeare's colleague Richard Burbage, in 1576 on lands of the old Holywell Priory adjacent to Finsbury Fields, a playground and park area just north of the city walls. It had the advantage of being outside the city's jurisdiction and yet was near enough to be easily accessible. Soon after The Theatre was opened, another playhouse called The Curtain was erected in the same neighborhood. Both of these playhouses had open courtyards and were probably polygonal in shape.

About the time The Curtain opened, Richard Farrant, Master of the Children of the Chapel Royal at Windsor and of St. Paul's, conceived the idea of opening a "private" theatre in the old monastery buildings of the Blackfriars, not far from St. Paul's Cathedral in the heart of the city. This theatre was ostensibly to train the choirboys in plays for presentation at Court, but Farrant managed to present plays to paying audiences and achieved considerable success until aristocratic neighbors complained and had the theatre closed. This first Blackfriars Theatre was significant, however, because it popularized the boy actors in a professional way and it paved the way for a second theatre in the Blackfriars, which Shakespeare's company took over more than thirty years later. By the last years of the sixteenth century, London had at least six professional theatres and still others were erected during the reign of James I.

The Globe Theatre, the playhouse that most people connect with Shakespeare, was erected early in 1599 on the Bankside, the area across the Thames from the city. Its construction had a dramatic beginning, for on the night of December 28, 1598, James Burbage's sons, Cuthbert and Richard, gathered together a crew who tore down the old theatre in Holywell and carted the timbers across the river to a site that they had chosen for a new playhouse. The reason for this clandestine operation was a row with the landowner over the lease to the Holywell property. The site chosen for the Globe was another playground outside of the city's jurisdiction, a region of somewhat unsavory character. Not far away was the Bear Garden, an amphitheatre devoted to the baiting of bears and bulls. This was also the region occupied by many houses of ill fame licensed by the Bishop of Winchester and the source of substantial revenue to him. But it was easily accessible either from London Bridge or by means of the cheap boats operated by the London watermen, and it had the great advantage of being beyond the authority of the Puritanical aldermen of London, who frowned on plays because they lured apprentices from work, filled their heads with improper ideas, and generally exerted a bad influence. The aldermen also complained that the crowds drawn together in the theatre helped to spread the plague.

The Globe was the handsomest theatre up to its time. It was a large building, apparently octagonal in shape, and open like its predecessors to the sky in the center, but capable of seating a large audience in its covered balconies. To erect and operate the Globe, the Burbages organized a syndicate composed of the leading members of the dramatic company, of which Shakespeare was a member. Since it was open to the weather and depended on natural light, plays had to be given in the afternoon.

This caused no hardship in the long afternoons of an English summer, but in the winter the weather was a great handicap and discouraged all except the hardiest. For that reason, in 1608 Shakespeare's company was glad to take over the lease of the second Blackfriars Theatre, a substantial, roomy hall reconstructed within the framework of the old monastery building. This theatre was protected from the weather and its stage was artificially lighted by chandeliers of candles. This became the winter playhouse for Shakespeare's company and at once proved so popular that the congestion of traffic created an embarrassing problem. Stringent regulations had to be made for the movement of coaches in the vicinity. Shakespeare's company continued to use the Globe during the summer months. In 1613 a squib fired from a cannon during a performance of *Henry VIII* fell on the thatched roof and the Globe burned to the ground. The next year it was rebuilt.

London had other famous theatres. The Rose, just west of the Globe, was built by Philip Henslowe, a semiliterate denizen of the Bankside, who became one of the most important theatrical owners and producers of the Tudor and Stuart periods. What is more important for historians, he kept a detailed account book, which provides much of our information about theatrical history in his time. Another famous theatre on the Bankside was the Swan, which a Dutch priest, Johannes de Witt, visited in 1596. The crude drawing of the stage which he made was copied by his friend Arend van Buchell; it is one of the important pieces of contemporary evidence for theatrical construction. Among the other theatres, the Fortune, north of the city, on Golding Lane, and the Red Bull, even farther away from the city, off St. John's Street, were the most popular. The Red Bull, much frequented by apprentices, favored sensational and sometimes rowdy plays.

The actors who kept all of these theatres going were organized into companies under the protection of some noble patron. Traditionally actors had enjoyed a low reputation. In some of the ordinances they were classed as vagrants; in the phraseology of the time, "rogues, vagabonds, sturdy beggars, and common players" were all listed together as undesirables. To escape penalties often meted out to these characters, organized groups of actors managed to gain the protection of various personages of high degree. In the later years of Elizabeth's reign, a group flourished under the name of the Queen's Men; another group had the protection of the Lord Admiral and were known as the Lord Admiral's Men. Edward Alleyn, son-in-law of Philip Henslowe, was the leading spirit in the Lord Admiral's Men. Besides the adult companies, troupes of boy actors from time to time also enjoyed considerable popularity. Among these were the Children of Paul's and the Children of the Chapel Royal.

The company with which Shakespeare had a long association had for its first patron Henry Carey,

Lord Hunsdon, the Lord Chamberlain, and hence
they were known as the Lord Chamberlain's Men.
After the accession of James I, they became the
King's Men. This company was the great rival of
the Lord Admiral's Men, managed by Henslowe
and Alleyn.

All was not easy for the players in Shakespeare's
time, for the aldermen of London were always
eager for an excuse to close up the Blackfriars and
any other theatres in their jurisdiction. The theatres
outside the jurisdiction of London were not im-
mune from interference, for they might be shut up
by order of the Privy Council for meddling in poli-
tics or for various other offenses, or they might be
closed in time of plague lest they spread infection.
During plague times, the actors usually went on
tour and played the provinces wherever they could
find an audience. Particularly frightening were the
plagues of 1592–1594 and 1613 when the theatres
closed and the players, like many other Londoners,
had to take to the country.

Though players had a low social status, they enjoyed great popularity, and one of the favorite
forms of entertainment at court was the performance of plays. To be commanded to perform at
court conferred great prestige upon a company of
players, and printers frequently noted that fact
when they published plays. Several of Shakespeare's
plays were performed before the sovereign, and
Shakespeare himself undoubtedly acted in some of
these plays.

REFERENCES FOR FURTHER READING

Many readers will want suggestions for further reading about Shakespeare and his times. The literature in this field is enormous but a few references will serve as guides to further study. A simple and useful little book is Gerald Sanders, *A Shakespeare Primer* (New York, 1950). *A Companion to Shakespeare Studies,* edited by Harley Granville-Barker and G. B. Harrison (Cambridge, Eng., 1934), is a valuable guide. More detailed but still not so voluminous as to be confusing is Hazelton Spencer, *The Art and Life of William Shakespeare* (New York, 1940), which, like Sanders' handbook, contains a brief annotated list of useful books on various aspects of the subject. The most recent concise handbook of facts about Shakespeare is Gerald E. Bentley, *Shakespeare: A Biographical Handbook* (New Haven, 1961). The most detailed and scholarly work providing complete factual information about Shakespeare is Sir Edmund Chambers, *William Shakespeare: A Study of Facts and Problems* (2 vols., Oxford, 1930). For detailed, factual information about the Elizabethan and seventeenth-century stages, the definitive reference works are Sir Edmund Chambers, *The Elizabethan Stage* (4 vols., Oxford, 1923) and Gerald E. Bentley, *The Jacobean and Caroline Stage* (5 vols., Oxford, 1941–1956). Alfred Harbage, *Shakespeare's Audience* (New York, 1941) throws light on the nature and tastes for the customers for whom Elizabethan dramatists wrote.

Although specialists disagree about the details of stage construction, the reader will find essential information in John C. Adams, *The Globe Playhouse: Its Design and Equipment* (Cambridge, Mass., 1942; 2nd ed., rev., New York, 1961). A model of the Globe playhouse by Dr. Adams is on permanent exhibition in the Folger Shakespeare Library in Washington, D.C. An excellent description of the architecture of the Globe is Irwin Smith, *Shakespeare's Globe Playhouse: A Modern Reconstruction in Text and Scale Drawings Based upon the Reconstruction of the Globe by John Cranford Adams* (New York, 1956). Another recent study of the physical characteristics of the Globe is C. Walter Hodges, *The Globe Restored* (London, 1953). An easily read history of the early theatres is J. Q. Adams, *Shakespearean Playhouses: A History of English Theatres from the Beginnings to the Restoration* (Boston, 1917). Bernard Beckerman, *Shakespeare at the Globe, 1599–1609* (New York, 1962), considers, in addition to the physical conditions of Shakespeare's theatre, theatrical conventions and acting styles of the period.

The following titles on theatrical history will provide information about Shakespeare's plays in later periods: Alfred Harbage, *Theatre for Shakespeare* (Toronto, 1955); Esther Cloudman Dunn, *Shakespeare in America* (New York, 1939); George C. D. Odell, *Shakespeare from Betterton to Irving* (2 vols.,

London, 1931); Arthur Colby Sprague, *Shakespeare and the Actors: The Stage Business in His Plays (1660–1905)* (Cambridge, Mass., 1944) and *Shakespearian Players and Performances* (Cambridge, Mass., 1953); Leslie Hotson, *The Commonwealth and Restoration Stage* (Cambridge, Mass., 1928); Alwin Thaler, *Shakspere to Sheridan: A Book About the Theatre of Yesterday and To-day* (Cambridge, Mass., 1922); Ernest Bradlee Watson, *Sheridan to Robertson: A Study of the 19th-Century London Stage* (Cambridge, Mass., 1926). Enid Welsford, *The Court Masque* (Cambridge, Mass., 1927) is an excellent study of the characteristics of this form of entertainment.

Harley Granville-Barker, *Prefaces to Shakespeare* (5 vols., London, 1927–1948) provides stimulating critical discussion of the plays. An older classic of criticism is Andrew C. Bradley, *Shakespearean Tragedy: Lectures on Hamlet, Othello, King Lear, Macbeth* (London, 1904), which is now available in an inexpensive reprint (New York, 1955). Thomas M. Parrott, *Shakespearean Comedy* (New York, 1949) is scholarly and readable. Also useful are George S. Gordon, *Shakespearian Comedy and Other Studies* (London and New York, 1945) and John R. Brown, *Shakespeare and His Comedies* (London, 1957). Shakespeare's dramatizations of English history are examined in E. M. W. Tillyard, *Shakespeare's History Plays* (London, 1948), and Lily Bess Campbell, *Shakespeare's "Histories," Mirrors of Elizabethan Policy* (San Marino, Calif., 1947) contains a more technical discussion of the same subject. Although

Edward Dowden's criticism is no longer fashionable, his *Shakspere: A Critical Study of His Mind and Art* (London, 1901; paperback reprint, 1962) is sensitive and often sensible.

Comments on the "sociological" aspects of *The Taming of the Shrew* may be found in John Bailey, *Shakespeare* (London, 1929) and in John Masefield, *William Shakespeare* (New York, 1911). Detailed discussions of the possible relation of Shakespeare's *Shrew* to *The Taming of a Shrew* appear in the Arden edition of the play edited by R. W. Bond (London, 1904) and John Munro's edition in *The London Shakespeare*.

The question of the authenticity of Shakespeare's plays arouses perennial attention. A book that demolishes the notion of hidden cryptograms in the plays is William F. Friedman and Elizebeth S. Friedman, *The Shakespearean Ciphers Examined* (New York, 1957). A succinct account of the various absurdities advanced to suggest the authorship of a multitude of candidates other than Shakespeare will be found in R. C. Churchill's *Shakespeare and His Betters* (Bloomington, Ind., 1959) and Frank W. Wadsworth, *The Poacher from Stratford: A Partial Account of the Controversy over the Authorship of Shakespeare's Plays* (Berkeley, Calif., 1958). An essay on the curious notions in the writings of the anti-Shakespeareans is that by Louis B. Wright, "The Anti-Shakespeare Industry and the Growth of Cults," *The Virginia Quarterly Review*, XXXV (1959), 289-303. Another recent discussion of the subject, *The Authorship of Shakespeare,* by James G. McManaway (Washington, 1962), presents all the evidence from contemporary records to prove the identity of Shakespeare the actor-playwright with Shakespeare of Stratford.

Reprints of some of the sources of Shakespeare's plays can be found in *Shakespeare's Library* (2 vols., 1850), edited by John Payne Collier, and *The Shakespeare Classics* (12 vols., 1907–1926), edited by Israel Gollancz. Geoffrey Bullough, *Narrative and Dramatic Sources of Shakespeare* contains the most recent reprinting of the source narratives (4 volumes published to date, covering the comedies written before 1603 and the history plays). For discussion of Shakespeare's use of his sources see Kenneth Muir, *Shakespeare's Sources: Comedies and Tragedies* (London, 1957). Thomas M. Cranfill has edited a facsimile reprint of Barnabe Rich's *Farewell to Military Profession (1581)* (Austin, Tex., 1959), which contains stories that Shakespeare probably used for several of his plays.

Interesting pictures as well as new information about Shakespeare will be found in F. E. Halliday, *Shakespeare, a Pictorial Biography* (London, 1956). Allardyce Nicoll, *The Elizabethans* (Cambridge, Eng., 1957) contains a variety of illustrations.

A brief, clear, and accurate account of Tudor history is S. T. Bindoff, *The Tudors,* in the Penguin series. A readable general history is G. M. Trevelyan, *The History of England,* first published in 1926 and available in many editions. G. M. Trevelyan, *English Social History,* first published in

1942 and also available in many editions, provides fascinating information about England in all periods. Sir John Neale, *Queen Elizabeth* (London, 1934) is the best study of the great Queen. Various aspects of life in the Elizabethan period are treated in Louis B. Wright, *Middle-Class Culture in Elizabethan England* (Chapel Hill, N.C.; reprinted Ithaca, N.Y., 1958). *Shakespeare's England: An Account of the Life and Manners of His Age,* edited by Sidney Lee and C. T. Onions (2 vols., Oxford, 1916), provides a large amount of information on many aspects of life in the Elizabeth period. Additional information will be found in Muriel St. C. Byrne, *Elizabeth Life in Town and Country* (London, 1925; rev. ed., 1954; paperback, N.Y., 1961).

The Folger Shakespeare Library is currently publishing a series of illustrated pamphlets on various aspects of English life in the sixteenth and seventeenth centuries. The following titles have been published: Dorothy E. Mason, *Music in Elizabethan England;* Craig R. Thompson, *The English Church in the Sixteenth Century;* Louis B. Wright, *Shakespeare's Theatre and the Dramatic Tradition;* Giles E. Dawson, *The Life of William Shakespeare;* Virginia A. LaMar, *English Dress in the Age of Shakespeare;* Craig R. Thompson, *The Bible in English, 1525–1611, The English Church in the Sixteenth Century, Schools in Tudor England,* and *Universities in Tudor England;* Lilly C. Stone, *English Sports and Recreations;* Conyers Read, *The Government of England under Elizabeth;* Virginia A. LaMar, *Travel and Roads in England;* John R. Hale,

The Art of War and Renaissance England; Albert J. Schmidt, *The Yeoman in Tudor and Stuart England;* James G. McManaway, *The Authorship of Shakespeare;* and Boies Penrose, *Tudor and Early Stuart Voyaging.*

[*Dramatis Personae*

A *Lord*.

Christopher Sly, a Beggar.

Hostess, Page, Players, Huntsmen, and *Servants*.

} persons in the Induction.

Baptista Minola, a gentleman of Padua.

Vincentio, a merchant of Pisa.

Lucentio, son to *Vincentio*, in love with *Bianca*.

Petruchio, a gentleman of Verona, suitor to *Katherina*.

Gremio,
Hortensio, } suitors to *Bianca*.

Tranio,
Biondello, } servants to *Lucentio*.

Grumio,
Curtis, } servants to *Petruchio*.

A *Pedant*.

Katherina, the shrew,
Bianca, } daughters to *Baptista*.

Widow.

Tailor, Haberdasher, and *Servants* attending on *Baptista* and *Petruchio*.

SCENE: *Padua, and Petruchio's country house*.]

THE
TAMING OF
THE SHREW

INDUCTION

[Ind. i.] Christopher Sly, a drunken beggar, staggers from an alehouse, pursued by the hostess, who threatens to call a constable. A nobleman, hunting with his servants, discovers the drunkard asleep and determines to have some sport at his expense. The servants are ordered to transport Sly to the nobleman's house, place him in a luxurious bed, and convince him that he is a great person who has been ill and out of his mind. The timely arrival of players, whom the lord engages to perform a comedy before Sly, furthers the stratagem.

⸻

1. **feeze:** beat; drive away; "fix."

4–5. **Richard Conqueror:** an error for William the Conqueror; **paucas pallabris:** Spanish *pocas palabras* (few words); "say no more."

5–6. **let the world slide:** a cant phrase expressing unconcern; **Sessa:** probably from French *cessez* (cease); "have done."

9–10. **denier:** a small coin, valued at one tenth of an English penny; **Go by, Jeronimy, go to thy cold bed and warm thee:** the phrase echoes two passages from Thomas Kyd's *The Spanish Tragedy* (III.xii.31 and II.v.i).

11–2. **thirdborough:** constable.

16. **tender:** care for.

Induction

Scene I. [Before an alehouse on a heath.]

Enter Beggar [Christopher Sly] and Hostess.

Sly. I'll feeze you, in faith.

Hos. A pair of stocks, you rogue!

Sly. Y'are a baggage; the Slys are no rogues. Look
in the chronicles; we came in with Richard Conqueror. Therefore, *paucas pallabris;* let the world   5
slide. Sessa!

Hos. You will not pay for the glasses you have
burst?

Sly. No, not a denier. Go by, Jeronimy, go to thy
cold bed and warm thee.   10

Hos. I know my remedy: I must go fetch the thirdborough.   [*Exit.*]

Sly. Third or fourth or fifth borough, I'll answer
him by law. I'll not budge an inch, boy; let him come,
and kindly.   *Falls asleep.*   15

*Wind horns. Enter a Lord from hunting, with his
Train.*

Lord. Huntsman, I charge thee, tender well my
hounds;

1

18. **Broach:** bleed. This is Dover Wilson's emendation of the word "Brach" in the Folio. "Brach" means "bitch," but the context seems to call for a verb; **embossed:** exhausted.

21. **coldest fault:** a **fault** is the loss of the quarry's scent; the **coldest fault** would be the faintest scent.

24. **at the merest loss:** when the loss of the scent was complete.

39. **practice:** play a trick.

43. **brave:** splendid.

A huntsman. From Ferdinando Bertelli, *Omnium fere gentium* (1563).

2

Broach Merriman, the poor cur is embossed, ~~bleed~~

And couple Clowder with the deep-mouthed brach.

Sawst thou not, boy, how Silver made it good 20

At the hedge corner in the coldest fault? ~~scent~~

I would not lose the dog for twenty pound.

   1. Hunt. Why, Bellman is as good as he, my lord;

He cried upon it at the merest loss

And twice today picked out the dullest scent. 25

Trust me, I take him for the better dog.

   Lord. Thou art a fool; if Echo were as fleet,

I would esteem him worth a dozen such.

But sup them well and look unto them all.

Tomorrow I intend to hunt again. 30

   1. Hunt. I will, my lord.

   Lord. What's here? one dead or drunk? See, doth
     he breathe?

   2. Hunt. He breathes, my lord. Were he not warmed
     with ale 35

This were a bed but cold to sleep so soundly.

   Lord. O monstrous beast! how like a swine he lies!

Grim death, how foul and loathsome is thine image!

Sirs, I will practice on this drunken man.

What think you, if he were conveyed to bed, 40

Wrapped in sweet clothes, rings put upon his fingers,

A most delicious banquet by his bed,

And brave attendants near him when he wakes,

Would not the beggar then forget himself?

   1. Hunt. Believe me, lord, I think he cannot choose. 45

   2. Hunt. It would seem strange unto him when he
     waked.

61. **diaper:** napkin.

69. **Sly:** an addition suggested by Samuel Johnson. The Folio reads "when he says he is, say . . ."

71. **kindly:** naturally.

72. **passing:** exceedingly.

73. **husbanded:** managed; **modesty:** moderation; i.e., without exaggeration.

76. **As:** so that.

Hounds at the hunt. From George Turberville, *The Noble Art of Venery* (1575).

3

Lord. Even as a flatt'ring dream or worthless fancy.
Then take him up, and manage well the jest.
Carry him gently to my fairest chamber,   50
And hang it round with all my wanton pictures;
Balm his foul head in warm distilled waters,
And burn sweet wood to make the lodging sweet.
Procure me music ready when he wakes,
To make a dulcet and a heavenly sound;   55
And if he chance to speak be ready straight,
And with a low submissive reverence
Say, "What is it your Honor will command?"
Let one attend him with a silver basin
Full of rose water and bestrewed with flowers;   60
Another bear the ewer, the third a diaper,
And say, "Will't please your Lordship cool your
    hands?"
Some one be ready with a costly suit
And ask him what apparel he will wear;   65
Another tell him of his hounds and horse
And that his lady mourns at his disease.
Persuade him that he hath been lunatic;
And when he says he's Sly, say that he dreams,
For he is nothing but a mighty lord.   70
This do, and do it kindly, gentle sirs.
It will be pastime passing excellent,
If it be husbanded with modesty.
   1. Hunt. My lord, I warrant you we will play our
       part,   75
As he shall think by our true diligence
He is no less than what we say he is.

79. **each one to his office:** let each perform his allotted role.

81. **Belike:** probably.

84. **An't:** if it.

90. **A Player:** the Folio text reads, in place of "A Player," "Sincklo," the name of an actor in Shakespeare's company.

91. **duty:** respectful service.

97. **Soto:** a character in some play that perhaps was the prototype of John Fletcher's *Women Pleased*, though it is not known to have been acted, in the form that has survived, until 1619.

99. **in happy time:** opportunely.

Lord. Take him up gently, and to bed with him;
And each one to his office when he wakes.
               [*They carry out Sly.*] *Sound trumpets.*
Sirrah, go see what trumpet 'tis that sounds: 80
                         [*Exit Servingman.*]
Belike some noble gentleman that means,
Traveling some journey, to repose him here.

[*Re-*]*enter Servingman.*

How now! who is it?
     Ser.   An't please your Honor, players
That offer service to your Lordship.   85
     Lord. Bid them come near.

Enter Players.

                    Now, fellows, you are welcome.
Players. We thank your Honor.
     Lord. Do you intend to stay with me tonight?
A Player. So please your Lordship to accept our   90
     duty.
     Lord. With all my heart. This fellow I remember
Since once he played a farmer's eldest son:
'Twas where you wooed the gentlewoman so well.
I have forgot your name; but sure that part   95
Was aptly fitted and naturally performed.
     A Player. I think 'twas Soto that your Honor means.
     Lord. 'Tis very true: thou didst it excellent.
Well, you are come to me in happy time,

100. **The rather:** all the more so; **for:** because.

103. **modesties:** self-controls.

106. **some merry passion:** a fit of uncontrollable laughter.

111. **antic:** buffoon.

112. **buttery:** a storage room for beverages.

114. **want:** lack.

116. **in all suits like a lady:** as befits a lady in every particular.

The rather for I have some sport in hand   100
Wherein your cunning can assist me much.
There is a lord will hear you play tonight;
But I am doubtful of your modesties,
Lest, overeyeing of his odd behavior—
For yet His Honor never heard a play—   105
You break into some merry passion
And so offend him; for I tell you, sirs,
If you should smile he grows impatient.
   A Player. Fear not, my lord, we can contain our-
     selves   110
Were he the veriest antic in the world.
   Lord. Go, sirrah, take them to the buttery
And give them friendly welcome every one.
Let them want nothing that my house affords.
                   Exit one with the Players.
Sirrah, go you to Barthol'mew my page   115
And see him dressed in all suits like a lady;
That done, conduct him to the drunkard's chamber
And call him "madam"; do him obeisance.
Tell him from me—as he will win my love—
He bear himself with honorable action   120
Such as he hath observed in noble ladies
Unto their lords, by them accomplished.
Such duty to the drunkard let him do
With soft low tongue and lowly courtesy,
And say, "What is't your Honor will command   125
Wherein your lady and your humble wife
May show her duty and make known her love?"
And then, with kind embracements, tempting kisses,

132. **him:** himself.

136. **shift:** trick.

137. **close:** secretly.

138. **in despite:** involuntarily.

139. **dispatched:** executed.

141. **usurp:** assume.

147. **spleen:** the organ regarded as the source of laughter.

━━━━━━━━━━━━━━━━━━━━━━━━━━━━━━━━

[Ind. ii.] When Sly awakens, the servants offer him food and drink and fine clothing. Although Sly protests his real identity, the lord assures him that he is deluded. As a servant describes the sorrow of his wife, Sly begins to believe the fiction. The sight of his supposed wife, impersonated by a page, makes him amorous, but the page puts him off. The players arrive, and Sly agrees to have them perform a comedy.

And with declining head into his bosom,
Bid him shed tears, as being overjoyed   130
To see her noble lord restored to health,
Who for this seven years hath esteemed him
No better than a poor and loathsome beggar.
And if the boy have not a woman's gift
To rain a shower of commanded tears,   135
An onion will do well for such a shift,
Which, in a napkin being close conveyed,
Shall in despite enforce a watery eye.
See this dispatched with all the haste thou canst;
Anon I'll give thee more instructions.   140

                         Exit a Servingman.

I know the boy will well usurp the grace,
Voice, gait, and action of a gentlewoman.
I long to hear him call the drunkard "husband,"
And how my men will stay themselves from laughter,
When they do homage to this simple peasant,   145
I'll in to counsel them; haply my presence
May well abate the overmerry spleen,
Which otherwise would grow into extremes.

                                    [Exeunt.]

[Scene II. A bedchamber in the Lord's house.]

*Enter, aloft, the drunkard [Sly], with Attendants,
some with apparel, [others with] basin and ewer
and other appurtenances, and Lord.*

1. **small:** weak.

3. **sack:** sherry.

9. **conserves of beef:** salted beef.

15. **idle humor:** not a mere mood but an excess of a particular "humor" (secretion of the body) that has caused madness.

20. **Burton Heath:** identified as Barton-on-the-Heath, a village about sixteen miles from Stratford where lived Shakespeare's aunt, Joan Lambert.

21. **cardmaker:** i.e., maker of cards for combing wool.

23–4. **Wincot:** perhaps Wilmcot near Stratford.

25. **on the score:** i.e., on the cuff; indebted; **sheer ale:** ale alone.

26–7. **bestraught:** distracted.

Sly. For God's sake! a pot of small ale.

1. Ser. Will't please your Lordship drink a cup of
sack?

2. Ser. Will't please your Honor taste of these con-
serves?   5

3. Ser. What raiment will your Honor wear today?

Sly. I am Christophero Sly; call not me "Honor" nor
"Lordship." I ne'er drank sack in my life; and if you
give me any conserves, give me conserves of beef.
Ne'er ask me what raiment I'll wear, for I have no   10
more doublets than backs, no more stockings than
legs, nor no more shoes than feet: nay, sometime
more feet than shoes, or such shoes as my toes look
through the overleather.

Lord. Heaven cease this idle humor in your Honor!   15
O that a mighty man of such descent,
Of such possessions and so high esteem,
Should be infused with so foul a spirit!

Sly. What! would you make me mad? Am not I
Christopher Sly, old Sly's son, of Burton Heath; by   20
birth a peddler, by education a cardmaker, by trans-
mutation a bearherd, and now by present profession
a tinker? Ask Marian Hacket, the fat alewife of Wincot, if she know me not: if she say I am not fourteen
pence on the score for sheer ale, score me up for the   25
lyingest knave in Christendom. What! I am not bestraught: here's—

3. Ser. O, this it is that makes your lady mourn!

2. Ser. O, this is it that makes your servants droop!

34. **ancient thoughts:** former reasoning powers.

42. **Semiramis:** a legendary queen of Assyria, whom Ninus of the Pyramus and Thisbe story took to wife; she was reported to have had numerous lovers.

43. **bestrew the ground:** i.e., with sweet-smelling herbs, as was done before the passing of the sovereign.

44. **trapped:** ornamented with trappings.

48. **welkin:** sky.

50. **course:** pursue hares, for which sport greyhounds were used.

52. **breathed:** long-winded.

56. **Cytherea:** another name for Venus, from the island Cythera, one of the centers of her worship; **sedges:** rushes or grasses that grow near water.

57. **wanton:** frolic.

59. **Io:** Io, daughter of Inachus, fled the advances of Jove, but the god caused a mist to obscure the world, which halted her flight and enabled him to capture her (Ovid, *Metamorphoses*, bk. i).

Semiramis. From *Le microcosme, contenant divers tableaux de la vie humaine* (Amsterdam, n.d.).

8

Lord. Hence comes it that your kindred shuns your   30
  house,
As beaten hence by your strange lunacy.
O noble lord, bethink thee of thy birth,
Call home thy ancient thoughts from banishment,
And banish hence these abject lowly dreams.   35
Look how thy servants do attend on thee,
Each in his office ready at thy beck.
Wilt thou have music? Hark! Apollo plays,   *Music.*
And twenty caged nightingales do sing.
Or wilt thou sleep? We'll have thee to a couch   40
Softer and sweeter than the lustful bed
On purpose trimmed up for Semiramis.
Say thou wilt walk, we will bestrew the ground.
Or wilt thou ride? Thy horses shall be trapped,
Their harness studded all with gold and pearl.   45
Dost thou love hawking? Thou hast hawks will soar
Above the morning lark. Or wilt thou hunt?
Thy hounds shall make the welkin answer them
And fetch shrill echoes from the hollow earth.
  1. Ser. Say thou wilt course, thy greyhounds are as   50
    swift
As breathed stags; ay, fleeter than the roe.
  2. Ser. Dost thou love pictures? We will fetch thee
    straight
Adonis painted by a running brook,   55
And Cytherea all in sedges hid,
Which seem to move and wanton with her breath,
Even as the waving sedges play with wind.
  Lord. We'll show thee Io as she was a maid,

60. **surprised:** taken; overcome.

62–6. **Daphne . . . drawn:** Apollo's unsuccessful pursuit of the nymph Daphne is described in Ovid, *Metamorphoses*, bk. i.

66. **workmanly:** in workmanlike fashion; skillfully.

71. **envious:** hostile.

84. **wit:** reason.

88. **fay:** faith.

89. **of:** in.

Venus and Adonis. From *Stirpium insignium nobilitatis* (*datus circa* 1602). See line 55 above.

And how she was beguiled and surprised,   60
As lively painted as the deed was done.
   3. Ser. Or Daphne roaming through a thorny
     wood,
Scratching her legs that one shall swear she bleeds;
And at that sight shall sad Apollo weep,   65
So workmanly the blood and tears are drawn.
   Lord. Thou art a lord and nothing but a lord;
Thou hast a lady far more beautiful
Than any woman in this waning age.
   1. Ser. And till the tears that she hath shed for thee   70
Like envious floods o'errun her lovely face,
She was the fairest creature in the world;
And yet she is inferior to none.
   Sly. Am I a lord? And have I such a lady?
Or do I dream? Or have I dreamed till now?   75
I do not sleep; I see, I hear, I speak;
I smell sweet savors and I feel soft things:
Upon my life, I am a lord indeed
And not a tinker nor Christopher Sly.
Well, bring our lady hither to our sight;   80
And once again, a pot o' the smallest ale.
   2. Ser. Will't please your Mightiness to wash your
     hands?
O, how we joy to see your wit restored!
O, that once more you knew but what you are!   85
These fifteen years you have been in a dream,
Or, when you waked, so waked as if you slept.
   Sly. These fifteen years! By my fay, a goodly nap.
But did I never speak of all that time?

90. **idle:** foolish.

93. **house:** alehouse.

94. **leet:** manorial court at which offenses such as overpricing and selling short measures were judged.

95. **sealed:** stamped by an official to certify their capacities.

100. **reckoned up:** enumerated.

101. **Stephen Sly:** a man of this name was servant to William Combe of Warwickshire, a friend of Shakespeare's; **Greece:** possibly Greet, in Gloucestershire. It is believed that the names of people listed here may all belong to countrymen whom Shakespeare actually knew.

105. **amends:** recovery.

114. **goodman:** husband.

1. Ser. O, yes, my lord, but very idle words;   90
For though you lay here in this goodly chamber,
Yet would you say ye were beaten out of door,
And rail upon the hostess of the house,
And say you would present her at the leet
Because she brought stone jugs and no sealed quarts. 95
Sometimes you would call out for Cicely Hacket.
 Sly. Ay, the woman's maid of the house.
 3. Ser. Why, sir, you know no house nor no such
  maid,
Nor no such men as you have reckoned up,   100
As Stephen Sly, and old John Naps of Greece,
And Peter Turph, and Henry Pimpernell,
And twenty more such names and men as these
Which never were nor no man ever saw.
 Sly. Now, Lord be thanked for my good amends! 105
 All. Amen.

  Enter [the Page, as a] Lady, with Attendants.

 Sly. I thank thee; thou shalt not lose by it.
 Page. How fares my noble lord?
 Sly. Marry, I fare well; for here is cheer enough.
Where is my wife?   110
 Page. Here, noble lord: what is thy will with her?
 Sly. Are you my wife and will not call me "hus-
  band"?
My men should call me "lord": I am your goodman.
 Page. My husband and my lord, my lord and hus- 115
  band;

125. **abandoned:** banished.

135. **tarry:** delay.

142. **meet:** suitable.

143. **sadness hath congealed your blood:** melancholy had this effect, according to Elizabethan physiological theory.

I am your wife in all obedience.

   Sly. I know it well. What must I call her?

   Lord. Madam.

   Sly. Al'ce madam or Joan madam?   120

   Lord. Madam and nothing else: so lords call ladies.

   Sly. Madam wife, they say that I have dreamed

And slept above some fifteen year or more.

   Page. Ay, and the time seems thirty unto me,

Being all this time abandoned from your bed.   125

   Sly. 'Tis much. Servants, leave me and her alone.

Madam, undress you and come now to bed.

   Page. Thrice noble lord, let me entreat of you

To pardon me yet for a night or two,

Or, if not so, until the sun be set: 130

For your physicians have expressly charged,

In peril to incur your former malady,

That I should yet absent me from your bed.

I hope this reason stands for my excuse.

   Sly. Ay, it stands so that I may hardly tarry so long;   135

but I would be loath to fall into my dreams again:

I will therefore tarry in despite of the flesh and the

blood.

Enter a Messenger.

   Messenger. Your Honor's players, hearing your

     amendment,   140

Are come to play a pleasant comedy;

For so your doctors hold it very meet,

Seeing too much sadness hath congealed your blood,

148. **comonty:** Sly's error for "comedy."
149. **gambold:** gambol; caper.
152. **history:** i.e., tale.

And melancholy is the nurse of frenzy.
Therefore they thought it good you hear a play   145
And frame your mind to mirth and merriment,
Which bars a thousand harms and lengthens life.
  Sly. Marry, I will let them play it. Is not a comonty
a Christmas gambold or a tumbling trick?
  Page. No, my good lord, it is more pleasing stuff.   150
  Sly. What! household stuff?
  Page. It is a kind of history.
  Sly. Well, we'll see't. Come, madam wife, sit by my
    side
And let the world slip: we shall ne'er be younger.   155
                    [They sit and mark.]

THE
TAMING OF
THE SHREW

ACT I

[I. i.] The wealthy young Lucentio, with his servant Tranio, arrives in Padua to attend the university. He vows to apply himself to the study of virtue, although he does not intend to neglect more pleasurable pursuits. These two stand aside when Baptista Minola enters with his two daughters, Katherina and Bianca, and Bianca's suitors, Hortensio and Gremio. Baptista announces that he will allow no suit for Bianca's hand until his eldest daughter, Katherina, is married. The eavesdroppers, Lucentio and Tranio, are amazed at Katherina's display of temper, but Lucentio is immediately smitten with Bianca's sweetness and modesty. The disappointed suitors set out to find schoolmasters to instruct Baptista's daughters; they are hopeful that they may endear themselves to Baptista if they can prove helpful. Hortensio points out to Gremio, however, that their first maneuver should be to find a husband for the shrewish Katherina.

Ent. **Flourish:** a series of notes on a trumpet announcing the beginning of the performance.

2. **Padua, nursery of arts:** so called because of the university located there.

3. **for:** in.

7. **approved:** confirmed.

8. **breathe:** pause; **haply:** perhaps.

9. **ingenious:** intellectual.

10. **grave:** worthy and dignified.

15. **serve:** perform the requirements of.

19. **apply:** address myself to.

[*ACT I*]

[Scene I. Padua. A public place.]

Flourish. Enter Lucentio and his man Tranio.

  Luc. Tranio, since for the great desire I had
To see fair Padua, nursery of arts,
I am arrived for fruitful Lombardy,
The pleasant garden of great Italy,
And by my father's love and leave am armed   5
With his good will and thy good company,
My trusty servant, well approved in all,
Here let us breathe and haply institute
A course of learning and ingenious studies.
Pisa, renowned for grave citizens,   10
Gave me my being and my father first,
A merchant of great traffic through the world,
Vincentio, come of the Bentivolii.
Vincentio's son, brought up in Florence,
It shall become to serve all hopes conceived,   15
To deck his fortune with his virtuous deeds.
And therefore, Tranio, for the time I study,
Virtue and that part of philosophy
Will I apply that treats of happiness
By virtue specially to be achieved.   20
Tell me thy mind, for I have Pisa left

13

23. **plash:** pool.

26. **affected:** inclined.

31. **stocks:** senseless blocks.

32. **devote:** devoted; **checks:** moral restraints.

33. **As:** so that; **Ovid be an outcast:** the poet Ovid was exiled by the Emperor Augustus, ostensibly for the impropriety of his treatise on the art of love, but more likely for some knowledge of an escapade of the Emperor's daughter.

34. **Balk:** bandy.

36. **quicken:** stimulate.

38. **stomach:** taste.

40. **affect:** prefer.

41. **Gramercies:** many thanks.

View of Padua. From Pietro Bertelli, *Theatrum urbium Italicarum* (1599).

And am to Padua come, as he that leaves
A shallow plash to plunge him in the deep,
And with satiety seeks to quench his thirst.
 Tra. *Mi perdonato*, gentle master mine: 25
I am in all affected as yourself,
Glad that you thus continue your resolve
To suck the sweets of sweet philosophy.
Only, good master, while we do admire
This virtue and this moral discipline,   30
Let's be no stoics nor no stocks, I pray;
Or so devote to Aristotle's checks
As Ovid be an outcast quite abjured.
Balk logic with acquaintance that you have,
And practice rhetoric in your common talk;   35
Music and poesy use to quicken you;
The mathematics and the metaphysics,
Fall to them as you find your stomach serves you.
No profit grows where is no pleasure ta'en;
In brief, sir, study what you most affect.   40
 Luc. Gramercies, Tranio, well dost thou advise.
If, Biondello, thou wert come ashore,
We could at once put us in readiness
And take a lodging fit to entertain
Such friends as time in Padua shall beget.   45

*Enter Baptista with his two daughters, Katherina
and Bianca; Gremio, a Pantaloon; [and] Hortensio,
suitor to Bianca. Lucentio [and] Tranio stand by.*

But stay awhile: what company is this?
 Tra. Master, some show to welcome us to town.

55. **cart her:** transport her in an open cart to be subjected to shame, a punishment for both scolds and loose women.

58. **stale:** (1) butt, (2) prostitute; **mates:** fellows (contemptuously); also would-be husbands for Bianca.

63. **Iwis:** certainly.

66. **paint your face:** i.e., with bleeding scratches; or possibly, with shamefaced blushes.

70. **toward:** in prospect.

71. **froward:** perverse.

Bap. Gentlemen, importune me no farther,
For how I firmly am resolved you know;
That is, not to bestow my youngest daughter   50
Before I have a husband for the elder.
If either of you both love Katherina,
Because I know you well and love you well,
Leave shall you have to court her at your pleasure.
    Gre. To cart her rather; she's too rough for me.   55
There, there, Hortensio, will you any wife?
    Kat. I pray you, sir, is it your will
To make a stale of me amongst these mates?
    Hor. Mates, maid! How mean you that? No mates
        for you,   60
Unless you were of gentler, milder mold.
    Kat. I' faith, sir, you shall never need to fear;
Iwis it is not halfway to her heart;
But if it were, doubt not her care should be
To comb your noddle with a three-legged stool   65
And paint your face and use you like a fool.
    Hor. From all such devils, good Lord deliver us!
    Gre. And me too, good Lord!
    Tra. Husht, master! Here's some good pastime
        toward.   70
That wench is stark mad or wonderful froward.
    Luc. But in the other's silence do I see
Maid's mild behavior and sobriety.
Peace, Tranio!
    Tra. Well said, master; mum! and gaze your fill.   75
    Bap. Gentlemen, that I may soon make good
What I have said—Bianca, get you in:

80–1. **It is best/Put finger in the eye, an she knew why:** she ought to cry if she had the wit to appreciate her position.

82. **discontent:** unhappiness.

83. **subscribe:** submit.

86. **Minerva:** goddess of wisdom, patroness of the arts and trades; she was also believed to have invented musical instruments.

87. **strange:** unnatural in the sense of being unkind.

90. **mew her up:** confine her. Hawks kept for hunting were confined in structures called "mews."

100. **Prefer:** recommend; **cunning:** clever.

And let it not displease thee, good Bianca,
For I will love thee ne'er the less, my girl.
   Kat. A pretty pet! It is best   80
Put finger in the eye, an she knew why.
   Bia. Sister, content you in my discontent.
Sir, to your pleasure humbly I subscribe:
My books and instruments shall be my company,
On them to look and practice by myself.   85
   Luc. Hark, Tranio! thou mayst hear Minerva speak.
   Hor. Signior Baptista, will you be so strange?
Sorry am I that our good will effects
Bianca's grief.
   Gre.   Why will you mew her up,   90
Signior Baptista, for this fiend of hell,
And make her bear the penance of her tongue?
   Bap. Gentlemen, content ye; I am resolved.
Go in, Bianca.   *[Exit Bianca.]*
And for I know she taketh most delight   95
In music, instruments, and poetry,
Schoolmasters will I keep within my house
Fit to instruct her youth. If you, Hortensio,
Or, Signior Gremio, you, know any such,
Prefer them hither; for to cunning men   100
I will be very kind, and liberal
To mine own children in good bringing up;
And so, farewell. Katherina, you may stay,
For I have more to commune with Bianca.   *Exit.*
   Kat. Why, and I trust I may go too; may I not?   105
What! shall I be appointed hours, as though, belike,

110. **blow our nails:** a gesture of patient unconcern.

111–12. **our cake's dough on both sides:** proverbial: "Our plans have gone awry."

117. **brooked:** endured.

118. **parle:** consultation; **advice:** careful consideration.

123. **Marry:** verily (by the Virgin Mary).

127. **very a fool:** an absolute fool.

135. **high cross:** an elevated cross set in the market place or town center.

I knew not what to take and what to leave? Ha! *Exit.*

Gre. You may go to the devil's dam: your gifts are
so good, here's none will hold you. Their love is not
so great, Hortensio, but we may blow our nails to- 110
gether and fast it fairly out; our cake's dough on
both sides. Farewell: yet, for the love I bear my sweet
Bianca, if I can by any means light on a fit man to
teach her that wherein she delights, I will wish him
to her father. 115

Hor. So will I, Signior Gremio; but a word, I pray.
Though the nature of our quarrel yet never brooked
parle, know now, upon advice, it toucheth us both—
that we may yet again have access to our fair mistress
and be happy rivals in Bianca's love—to labor and 120
effect one thing specially.

Gre. What's that, I pray?

Hor. Marry, sir, to get a husband for her sister.

Gre. A husband! A devil.

Hor. I say, a husband. 125

Gre. I say, a devil. Thinkst thou, Hortensio, though
her father be very rich, any man is so very a fool to
be married to hell?

Hor. Tush, Gremio! Though it pass your patience
and mine to endure her loud alarums, why, man, 130
there be good fellows in the world, an a man could
light on them, would take her with all faults, and
money enough.

Gre. I cannot tell; but I had as lief take her dowry
with this condition: to be whipped at the high cross 135
every morning.

142–43. **have to't afresh:** let's renew the assault; **Happy man be his dole:** may the winner be a happy man.

154. **love in idleness:** a pun on one designation for the pansy, the flower used in *A Midsummer Night's Dream* to evoke love.

157. **Anna:** the sister and confidante of Dido, Queen of Carthage, in Virgil's *Aeneid*, bk. iv.

163. **rated from:** expelled by scolding.

Anna and Dido at Dido's funeral pyre. From Vergil, *Aeneid*, in *Works* (1537).

Hor. Faith, as you say, there's small choice in rot-
ten apples. But come; since this bar in law makes us
friends, it shall be so far forth friendly maintained,
till by helping Baptista's eldest daughter to a hus-   140
band we set his youngest free for a husband, and then
have to't afresh. Sweet Bianca! Happy man be his
dole! He that runs fastest gets the ring. How say you,
Signior Gremio?

Gre. I am agreed; and would I had given him the   145
best horse in Padua to begin his wooing that would
thoroughly woo her, wed her, and bed her, and rid
the house of her. Come on.

                Exeunt [Gremio and Hortensio.]

Tra. I pray, sir, tell me, is it possible
That love should of a sudden take such hold?   150

Luc. O Tranio! till I found it to be true
I never thought it possible or likely.
But see, while idly I stood looking on,
I found the effect of love in idleness,
And now in plainness do confess to thee,   155
That art to me as secret and as dear
As Anna to the Queen of Carthage was,
Tranio, I burn, I pine, I perish, Tranio,
If I achieve not this young modest girl.
Counsel me, Tranio, for I know thou canst;   160
Assist me, Tranio, for I know thou wilt.

Tra. Master, it is no time to chide you now;
Affection is not rated from the heart:
If love have touched you, nought remains but so,

165. Redime te captum quam queas minimo: "redeem yourself from captivity as cheaply as you can" The quotation is from Terence, *Eunuch.*, I.i.29, but Shakespeare's remembrance follows the quotation of it in William Lily's Latin grammar.

168. longly: lingeringly.

169. pith: essence.

171. daughter of Agenor: Europa, one of Jove's mistresses.

184. curst: ill-tempered; **shrewd:** shrewish; disagreeable.

188. Because: so that.

194. for my hand: I'll stake my hand.

Jove carrying off Europa. From Gabriel Simeoni, *La vita et Metamorfoseo d'Ovidio* (1559).

Redime te captum quam queas minimo.   165

   Luc. Gramercies, lad; go forward. This contents;
The rest will comfort, for thy counsel's sound.

   Tra. Master, you looked so longly on the maid,
Perhaps you marked not what's the pith of all.

   Luc. O, yes, I saw sweet beauty in her face,   170
Such as the daughter of Agenor had,
That made great Jove to humble him to her hand
When with his knees he kissed the Cretan strand.

   Tra. Saw you no more? Marked you not how her
      sister   175
Began to scold and raise up such a storm
That mortal ears might hardly endure the din?

   Luc. Tranio, I saw her coral lips to move,
And with her breath she did perfume the air.
Sacred and sweet was all I saw in her.   180

   Tra. Nay, then, 'tis time to stir him from his trance.
I pray, awake, sir; if you love the maid,
Bend thoughts and wits to achieve her. Thus it stands:
Her elder sister is so curst and shrewd
That till the father rid his hands of her,   185
Master, your love must live a maid at home;
And therefore has he closely mewed her up,
Because she will not be annoyed with suitors.

   Luc. Ah, tranio, what a cruel father's he!
But art thou not advised he took some care   190
To get her cunning schoolmasters to instruct her?

   Tra. Ay, marry, am I, sir; and now 'tis plotted.

   Luc. I have it, Tranio.

   Tra.   Master, for my hand,

195. **jump:** coincide.

203. **Keep house:** maintain hospitality.

205. **Basta:** enough; **I have it full:** I see the whole plan.

210. **port:** style of living.

218. **sith:** since.

Both our inventions meet and jump in one.   195
   Luc. Tell me thine first.
   Tra.   You will be schoolmaster
And undertake the teaching of the maid:
That's your device.
   Luc.   It is; may it be done?   200
   Tra. Not possible; for who shall bear your part
And be in Padua here Vincentio's son;
Keep house and ply his book, welcome his friends,
Visit his countrymen and banquet them?
   Luc. Basta, content thee; for I have it full.   205
We have not yet been seen in any house,
Nor can we be distinguished by our faces
For man or master. Then, it follows thus:
Thou shalt be master, Tranio, in my stead,
Keep house and port and servants as I should;   210
I will some other be—some Florentine,
Some Neapolitan, or meaner man of Pisa.
'Tis hatched and shall be so. Tranio, at once
Uncase thee; take my colored hat and cloak.
When Biondello comes he waits on thee;   215
But I will charm him first to keep his tongue.
   Tra. So had you need.
In brief, sir, sith it your pleasure is
And I am tied to be obedient—
For so your father charged me at our parting: 220
"Be serviceable to my son," quoth he,
Although I think 'twas in another sense—
I am content to be Lucentio,
Because so well I love Lucentio.

237. **count'nance:** semblance.

Luc. Tranio, be so, because Lucentio loves;   225
And let me be a slave, t'achieve that maid
Whose sudden sight hath thralled my wounded eye.
Here comes the rogue.

Enter Biondello.

                    Sirrah, where have you been?
Bio. Where have I been! Nay, how now! Where   230
    are you?
Master, has my fellow Tranio stol'n your clothes,
Or you stol'n his? or both? Pray, what's the news?
Luc. Sirrah, come hither: 'tis no time to jest,
And therefore frame your manners to the time.   235
Your fellow Tranio here, to save my life,
Puts my apparel and my count'nance on,
And I for my escape have put on his;
For in a quarrel since I came ashore
I killed a man and fear I was descried.   240
Wait you on him, I charge you, as becomes,
While I make way from hence to save my life.
You understand me?
Bio.   I, sir! ne'er a whit.
Luc. And not a jot of Tranio in your mouth.   245
Tranio is changed into Lucentio.
Bio. The better for him; would I were so too!
Tra. So could I, faith, boy, to have the next wish
    after,
That Lucentio indeed had Baptista's youngest   250
    daughter.

259. **rests:** remains.
S.D. after l. 261. **Presenters:** actors.
262. **mind:** heed.

━━━━━━━━━━━━━━━━━━━━━━━━━━━━━━━━━━━━

[**I. ii.**] Petruchio and his servant Grumio arrive in Padua, where Petruchio immediately seeks his friend Hortensio. Hortensio welcomes Petruchio with delight and at once suggests that he seek Katherina for his wife, explaining the drawback of her foul disposition but emphasizing the large dowry that will accompany her hand. Petruchio, undaunted by this description of Katherina, asks to be conducted to Baptista and his daughter as soon as possible. Hortensio, in return, asks Petruchio to introduce him, disguised, as a music teacher, so that he may court Bianca. In the meantime, Gremio, unaware of Lucentio's true identity, arranges to present him to Baptista as a schoolmaster to instruct Bianca in literature and deportment. At Baptista's house they all meet with Tranio (now disguised as Lucentio), who announces his intention of wooing Bianca himself. The three suitors for Bianca's hand agree to further Petruchio's suit for Katherina in order to free the younger daughter for one of them.

━━━━━━━━━━━━━━━━━━━━━━━━━━━━

3. **approved:** tried.
4. **trow:** believe.

But, sirrah, not for my sake, but your master's,
    I advise
You use your manners discreetly in all kind of com-
    panies.   255
When I am alone, why, then I am Tranio;
But in all places else your master Lucentio.
  Luc. Tranio, let's go.
One thing more rests that thyself execute,
To make one among these wooers: if you ask me why, 260
Sufficeth my reasons are both good and weighty.

                          Exeunt.

The Presenters above speak.

  1. Ser. My lord, you nod; you do not mind the play.
  Sly. Yes, by Saint Anne, do I. A good matter surely;
comes there any more of it?
  Page. My lord, 'tis but begun.   265
  Sly. 'Tis a very excellent piece of work, madam
lady: would 'twere done!   *They sit and mark.*

[Scene II. Padua. Before Hortensio's house.]

Enter Petruchio, and his man Grumio.

  Pet. Verona, for a while I take my leave
To see my friends in Padua; but of all
My best beloved and approved friend,
Hortensio; and I trow this is his house.
Here, sirrah Grumio; knock, I say.   5
  Gru. Knock, sir? whom should I knock? Is there

7. **rebused:** comic error for "abused."

8. **me:** i.e., for me (the ethical dative construction).

12. **pate:** head.

25. **Con tutto il cuore ben trovato:** welcome with all my heart.

26–7. **Alla nostra casa ben venuto, molto honorato signor mio Petruchio:** welcome to our house, my most honored Master Petruchio.

28. **compound:** settle.

View of Verona. From Pietro Bertelli, *Theatrum urbium Italicarum* (1599).

Any man has rebused your worship?

  Pet. Villain, I say, knock me here soundly.

  Gru. Knock you here, sir? Why, sir, what am I,
Sir, that I should knock you here, sir?   10

  Pet. Villain, I say, knock me at this gate,
And rap me well or I'll knock your knave's pate.

  Gru. My master is grown quarrelsome. I should
    knock you first,
And then I know after who comes by the worst.   15

  Pet. Will it not be?
Faith, sirrah, and you'll not knock, I'll ring it;
I'll try how you can *sol, fa*, and sing it.

                   He wrings him by the ears.

  Gru. Help, masters, help! my master is mad.

  Pet. Now, knock when I bid you, sirrah villain!   20

             Enter Hortensio.

  Hor. How now, what's the matter? My old friend
Grumio! and my good friend Petruchio! How do you
all at Verona?

  Pet. Signior Hortensio, come you to part the fray?
Con tutto il cuore ben trovato, may I say.   25

  *Hor. Alla nostra casa ben venuto, molto honorato
signor mio Petruchio.*
Rise, Grumio, rise; we will compound this quarrel.

  Gru. Nay, 'tis no matter, sir, what he 'leges in Latin.
If this be not a lawful cause for me to leave his serv-   30
ice, look you, sir: he bid me knock him and rap him
soundly, sir. Well, was it fit for a servant to use his

33–4. **two-and-thirty, a pip out:** a phrase, derived from the card game "Trentuno," having the cant meaning of being drunk; **pip:** a spot marking on a card.

46. **this':** this is a; **heavy:** distressing.

47. **ancient:** i.e., of long standing.

53. **in a few:** to be brief.

60. **come roundly to thee:** speak directly.

master so, being, perhaps, for aught I see, two-and-
thirty, a pip out?

Whom would to God, I had well knocked at first, 35
Then had not Grumio come by the worst.

   Pet. A senseless villain! Good Hortensio,
I bade the rascal knock upon your gate,
And could not get him for my heart to do it.

   Gru. Knock at the gate? O heavens! Spake you not 40
these words plain: "Sirrah, knock me here; rap me
here; knock me well; and knock me soundly"? And
come you now with "knocking at the gate"?

   Pet. Sirrah, be gone, or talk not, I advise you.

   Hor. Petruchio, patience; I am Grumio's pledge. 45
Why, this' a heavy chance 'twixt him and you,
Your ancient, trusty, pleasant servant Grumio.
And tell me now, sweet friend, what happy gale
Blows you to Padua here from old Verona?

   Pet. Such wind as scatters young men through the 50
    world
To seek their fortunes farther than at home,
Where small experience grows. But in a few,
Signior Hortensio, thus it stands with me:
Antonio, my father, is deceased 55
And I have thrust myself into this maze,
Happily to wive and thrive as best I may.
Crowns in my purse I have, and goods at home,
And so am come abroad to see the world.

   Hor. Petruchio, shall I then come roundly to thee 60
And wish thee to a shrewd ill-favored wife?
Thou'dst thank me but a little for my counsel,

69. **burden:** i.e., refrain; probably used loosely to mean the tune played for the dance.

70. **foul:** ugly; **Florentius' love:** Florentius in Gower's *Confessio Amantis* promised to marry an ugly hag in exchange for the answer to a riddle that would save his life. Chaucer's "Wife of Bath's Tale" has a similar theme.

71. **Sibyl:** the Cumaean sibyl. Apollo granted her as many years of life as there were grains of sand in a nearby pile.

80. **puppet:** doll; **aglet-baby:** perhaps "agate-baby"? Cf. *Henry IV, Part 2*, I.ii.17, which refers to carving on agate stones; **trot:** hag.

85. **that:** that which; what.

Apollo and the Cumaean Sibyl. From Gabriel Simeoni, *La vita et Metamorfoseo d'Ovidio* (1559).

And yet I'll promise thee she shall be rich,
And very rich; but thou'rt too much my friend,
And I'll not wish thee to her.   65

Pet. Signior Hortensio, 'twixt such friends as we
Few words suffice; and therefore, if thou know
One rich enough to be Petruchio's wife,
As wealth is burden of my wooing dance,
Be she as foul as was Florentius' love,   70
As old as Sibyl, and as curst and shrewd
As Socrates' Xanthippe, or a worse,
She moves me not, or not removes, at least,
Affection's edge in me, were she as rough
As are the swelling Adriatic seas.   75
I come to wive it wealthily in Padua;
If wealthily, then happily in Padua.

Gru. Nay, look you, sir, he tells you flatly what his
mind is; why, give him gold enough and marry him
to a puppet or an aglet-baby or an old trot with ne'er   80
a tooth in her head, though she have as many dis-
eases as two-and-fifty horses: why, nothing comes
amiss so money comes withal.

Hor. Petruchio, since we are stepped thus far in,
I will continue that I broached in jest.   85
I can, Petruchio, help thee to a wife
With wealth enough, and young and beauteous,
Brought up as best becomes a gentlewoman.
Her only fault—and that is faults enough—
Is that she is intolerable curst   90
And shrewd and froward, so beyond all measure,
That were my state far worser than it is

97. **board:** attempt to capture.
107. **give you over:** have no more to do with you.
110. **A:** on; **and:** an, meaning "if."
113. **so:** something of that sort.
114. **rope tricks:** knavery.
115. **figure:** figure of speech.

I would not wed her for a mine of gold.

  Pet. Hortensio, peace! Thou knowst not gold's
    effect.   95
Tell me her father's name, and 'tis enough;
For I will board her though she chide as loud
As thunder when the clouds in autumn crack.

  Hor. Her father is Baptista Minola,
An affable and courteous gentleman;   100
Her name is Katherina Minola,
Renowned in Padua for her scolding tongue.

  Pet. I know her father, though I know not her;
And he knew my deceased father well.
I will not sleep, Hortensio, till I see her;   105
And therefore let me be thus bold with you,
To give you over at this first encounter
Unless you will accompany me thither.

  Gru. I pray you, sir, let him go while the humor
lasts. A my word, and she knew him as well as I do, 110
she would think scolding would do little good upon
him. She may perhaps call him half a score knaves or
so: why, that's nothing; and he begin once, he'll rail
in his rope tricks. I'll tell you what, sir, and she stand
him but a little, he will throw a figure in her face 115
and so disfigure her with it that she shall have no
more eyes to see withal than a cat. You know him
not, sir.

  Hor. Tarry, Petruchio, I must go with thee,
For in Baptista's keep my treasure is.   120
He hath the jewel of my life in hold,
His youngest daughter, beautiful Bianca,

128. **ta'en:** i.e., given.

133. **grace:** a favor.

134. **sober:** dark-colored. Scholars usually wore long gowns of black or some other dark color.

136. **Well seen:** proficient.

140. **Here's no knavery:** uttered ironically.

145. **proper:** handsome; well-set-up.

148. **at any hand:** at all events.

149. **read no other lectures to her:** give her no other instruction.

And her withholds from me and other more,
Suitors to her and rivals in my love,
Supposing it a thing impossible,   125
For those defects I have before rehearsed,
That ever Katherina will be wooed.
Therefore this order hath Baptista ta'en,
That none shall have access unto Bianca
Till Katherine the curst have got a husband.   130
    Gru. Katherine the curst!
A title for a maid of all titles the worst.
    Hor. Now shall my friend Petruchio do me grace
And offer me, disguised in sober robes,
To old Baptista as a schoolmaster   135
Well seen in music, to instruct Bianca,
That so I may, by this device, at least
Have leave and leisure to make love to her,
And unsuspected court her by herself.

Enter Gremio, and Lucentio disguised [as Cambio].

    Gru. Here's no knavery! See, to beguile the old 140
folks, how the young folks lay their heads together!
Master, master, look about you. Who goes there, ha?
    Hor. Peace, Grumio! it is the rival of my love.
Petruchio, stand by awhile.
    Gru. A proper stripling, and an amorous!   145
    Gre. O, very well; I have perused the note.
Hark you, sir; I'll have them very fairly bound:
All books of love, see that at any hand;
And see you read no other lectures to her.
You understand me. Over and beside   150

152. **mend:** better; supplement; **largess:** gift.
157. **stand you so assured:** be assured of it.
158. **as:** as if; **in place:** present.
162. **woodcock:** fool.
179. **bags:** moneybags.
180. **vent:** express.

Signior Baptista's liberality,
I'll mend it with a largess. Take your paper too,
And let me have them very well perfumed,
For she is sweeter than perfume itself
To whom they go to. What will you read to her? 155
  Luc. Whate'er I read to her, I'll plead for you
As for my patron, stand you so assured,
As firmly as yourself were still in place;
Yea, and perhaps with more successful words
Than you, unless you were a scholar, sir.   160
  Gre. O, this learning, what a thing it is!
  Gru. O, this woodcock, what an ass it is!
  Pet. Peace, sirrah!
  Hor. Grumio, mum! God save you, Signior Gremio!
  Gre. And you are well met, Signior Hortensio. 165
Trow you whither I am going? To Baptista Minola.
I promised to inquire carefully
About a schoolmaster for the fair Bianca,
And, by good fortune, I have lighted well
On this young man; for learning and behavior   170
Fit for her turn; well read in poetry
And other books, good ones, I warrant ye.
  Hor. 'Tis well; and I have met a gentleman
Hath promised me to help me to another,
A fine musician to instruct our mistress;   175
So shall I no whit be behind in duty
To fair Bianca, so beloved of me.
  Gre. Beloved of me, and that my deeds shall prove.
  Gru. And that his bags shall prove.
  Hor. Gremio, 'tis now no time to vent our love. 180

182. **indifferent:** equally.
184. **Upon agreement:** on terms.
197. **stomach:** taste; courage.

Listen to me, and if you speak me fair
I'll tell you news indifferent good for either.
Here is a gentleman whom by chance I met,
Upon agreement from us to his liking,
Will undertake to woo curst Katherine;   185
Yea, and to marry her if her dowry please.
    Gre. So said, so done, is well.
Hortensio, have you told him all her faults?
    Pet. I know she is an irksome, brawling scold:
If that be all, masters, I hear no harm.   190
    Gre. No, sayst me so, friend? What countryman?
    Pet. Born in Verona, old Antonio's son:
My father dead, my fortune lives for me;
And I do hope good days and long to see.
    Gre. O, sir, such a life, with such a wife, were 195
        strange!
But if you have a stomach, to't a God's name;
You shall have me assisting you in all.
But will you woo this wildcat?
    Pet.   Will I live?   200
    Gru. [*Aside*] Will he woo her? Ay, or I'll hang her.
    Pet. Why came I hither but to that intent?
Think you a little din can daunt mine ears?
Have I not in my time heard lions roar?
Have I not heard the sea, puffed up with winds,   205
Rage like an angry boar chafed with sweat?
Have I not heard great ordnance in the field
And heaven's artillery thunder in the skies?
Have I not in a pitched battle heard
Loud larums, neighing steeds, and trumpets' clang? 210

214. **fear:** frighten; **bugs:** bogeymen.

220. **charge:** expense.

S.D. after l. 223. **brave:** bravely (splendidly) dressed.

225. **readiest:** nearest.

And do you tell me of a woman's tongue,
That gives not half so great a blow to hear
As will a chestnut in a farmer's fire?
Tush, tush! fear boys with bugs.

   Gru. [*Aside*]   For he fears none.   215
   Gre. Hortensio, hark:
This gentleman is happily arrived,
My mind presumes, for his own good and ours.

   Hor. I promised we would be contributors,
And bear his charge of wooing, whatsoe'er.   220

   Gre. And so we will, provided that he win her.

   Gru. [*Aside*] I would I were as sure of a good
    dinner.

Enter Tranio [as Lucentio], brave, and Biondello.

   Tra. Gentlemen, God save you! If I may be bold,
Tell me, I beseech you, which is the readiest way   225
To the house of Signior Baptista Minola?

   Bio. He that has the two fair daughters: is't he you
    mean?

   Tra. Even he, Biondello.

   Gre. Hark you, sir; you mean not her to—   230

   Tra. Perhaps, him and her, sir; what have you to
    do?

   Pet. Not her that chides, sir, at any hand, I pray.

   Tra. I love no chiders, sir. Biondello, let's away.

   Luc. Well begun, Tranio.   235

   Hor.   Sir, a word ere you go:
Are you a suitor to the maid you talk of, yea or no?

   Tra. And if I be, sir, is it any offense?

246. **choice:** chosen.

248. **Softly:** take it easy.

254. **Leda's daughter:** Helen of Troy, daughter of Leda and Jove.

257. **Paris:** the handsome son of the King of Troy, who stole Helen from her husband, Menelaus.

259. **jade:** nag; inferior piece of horseflesh.

266. **let her go by:** pass her up.

268. **Alcides' twelve:** i.e., the twelve labors of Hercules. **Alcides** ("descendant of Alcaeus") is a Greek name for the hero.

Some of the labors of Hercules. From Ovid, *Metamorphoses* (1522).

Gre. No, if without more words you will get you
  hence.   240

Tra. Why, sir, I pray, are not the streets as free
For me as for you?

Gre.   But so is not she.

Tra. For what reason, I beseech you?

Gre. For this reason, if you'll know,   245
That she's the choice love of Signior Gremio.

Hor. That she's the chosen of Signior Hortensio.

Tra. Softly, my masters! If you be gentlemen,
Do me this right; hear me with patience.
Baptista is a noble gentleman,   250
To whom my father is not all unknown,
And were his daughter fairer than she is
She may more suitors have, and me for one.
Fair Leda's daughter had a thousand wooers;
Then well one more may fair Bianca have,   255
And so she shall; Lucentio shall make one,
Though Paris came in hope to speed alone.

Gre. What! this gentleman will outtalk us all.

Luc. Sir, give him head. I know he'll prove a jade.

Pet. Hortensio, to what end are all these words?   260

Hor. Sir, let me be so bold as ask you,
Did you yet ever see Baptista's daughter?

Tra. No, sir; but hear I do that he hath two,
The one as famous for a scolding tongue
As is the other for beauteous modesty.   265

Pet. Sir, sir, the first's for me; let her go by.

Gre. Yea, leave that labor to great Hercules;
And let it be more than Alcides' twelve.

269. **in sooth:** truthfully.

276. **stead:** assist.

279. **whose hap shall be to have her:** whoever is lucky enough to win her.

280. **graceless:** ungracious.

283. **gratify:** reward.

286. **contrive:** pass the time.

287. **carouses:** deep draughts of liquor.

290. **motion:** suggestion.

293. **ben venuto:** welcomer; i.e., Hortensio will see that he is properly introduced.

Pet. Sir, understand you this of me in sooth:
The youngest daughter, whom you hearken for,   270
Her father keeps from all access of suitors,
And will not promise her to any man
Until the elder sister first be wed;
The younger then is free, and not before.

Tra. If it be so, sir, that you are the man   275
Must stead us all, and me amongst the rest;
And if you break the ice and do this feat,
Achieve the elder, set the younger free
For our access, whose hap shall be to have her
Will not so graceless be to be ingrate.   280

Hor. Sir, you say well, and well you do conceive;
And since you do profess to be a suitor,
You must, as we do, gratify this gentleman,
To whom we all rest generally beholding.

Tra. Sir, I shall not be slack: in sign whereof,   285
Please ye we may contrive this afternoon
And quaff carouses to our mistress' health,
And do as adversaries do in law,
Strive mightily, but eat and drink as friends.

Gru., Bio. O excellent motion! Fellows, let's be 290
    gone.

Hor. The motion's good indeed, and be it so:
Petruchio, I shall be your *ben venuto*.

                                        Exeunt.

THE
TAMING OF
THE SHREW

ACT II

[II. i.]   Petruchio, Lucentio, Gremio, Hortensio, and Tranio present themselves at Baptista's house. Petruchio declares himself a suitor for Katherina's hand and introduces Hortensio as Licio, a music master and mathematician, to instruct Baptista's daughters, while Gremio produces Lucentio as Cambio, a man learned in languages. Tranio, introducing himself as Lucentio, expresses his own interest in marrying Bianca and requests permission to court her. Baptista warns Petruchio of Katherina's shortcomings but agrees to give his consent if Petruchio can win her love. Katherina's first meeting with Petruchio seems to leave her unimpressed, but Petruchio vows that he is the man for her and will marry her whether she will or no. He reports to Baptista that he and Katherina have agreed very well and will be married the following Sunday. Baptista is dubious but he accepts Petruchio's word, and Petruchio leaves for Venice to prepare himself for the wedding. With Katherina's marriage apparently settled, Gremio and Tranio bid for Bianca's hand, and Tranio's inventory of worldly goods so far surpasses that of Gremio that Baptista promises Bianca to Tranio/Lucentio if he can bring assurance from his father, Vincentio, that the dowry promised will be paid. This leaves Tranio with the problem of providing a "supposed Vincentio" to give Baptista the necessary assurance.

<hr>

4. **gauds:** ornaments; jewels or trinkets.
15. **Minion:** spoiled darling.
19. **fair:** i.e., beautifully dressed.

[Scene I. Padua. A room in Baptista's house.]

Enter Katherina and Bianca [with her hands tied].

Bia. Good sister, wrong me not, nor wrong your-
    self,
To make a bondmaid and a slave of me;
That I disdain; but for these other gauds,
Unbind my hands, I'll pull them off myself,   5
Yea, all my raiment, to my petticoat;
Or what you will command me will I do,
So well I know my duty to my elders.
   Kat. Of all thy suitors, here I charge thee,
    tell   10
Whom thou lovest best; see thou dissemble not.
   Bia. Believe me, sister, of all the men alive
I never yet beheld that special face
Which I could fancy more than any other.
   Kat. Minion, thou liest. Is't not Hortensio?   15
   Bia. If you affect him, sister, here I swear
I'll plead for you myself but you shall have him.
   Kat. O, then, belike, you fancy riches more:
You will have Gremio to keep you fair.

29. **hilding:** wretch.

37. **dance barefoot:** a proverbial description of the state of a woman whose younger sister married before her.

38. **lead apes in hell:** proverbial: "Old maids lead apes in hell."

Bia. Is it for him you do envy me so?   20
Nay, then you jest, and now I well perceive
You have but jested with me all this while.
I prithee, sister Kate, untie my hands.

Kat. If that be jest then all the rest was so.
                                            Strikes her.

                Enter Baptista.

Bap. Why, how now, dame! Whence grows this   25
    insolence?
Bianca, stand aside. Poor girl! she weeps.
Go ply thy needle; meddle not with her.
For shame, thou hilding of a devilish spirit,
Why dost thou wrong her that did ne'er wrong thee? 30
When did she cross thee with a bitter word?

Kat. Her silence flouts me, and I'll be revenged.
                                    Flies after Bianca.

Bap. What! in my sight? Bianca, get thee in.
                                    Exit [Bianca].

Kat. What! will you not suffer me? Nay, now I
    see   35
She is your treasure, she must have a husband;
I must dance barefoot on her wedding day,
And, for your love to her, lead apes in hell.
Talk not to me: I will go sit and weep
Till I can find occasion of revenge.   *[Exit.]* 40

Bap. Was ever gentleman thus grieved as I?
But who comes here?

S.D. after l. 42. **mean:** baseborn.

51–2. **give me leave:** allow me to continue.

60. **for an entrance to my entertainment:** i.e., to earn my welcome.

A lute. From Roemer Visscher, *Sinnepoppen . . . 1614* (1949 edition).

*Enter Gremio, [with] Lucentio [(Cambio)] in the
habit of a mean man; Petruchio, with [Hortensio
(Licio) as a Musician; and] Tranio [(Lucentio)],
with his boy [Biondello] bearing a lute and books.*

Gre. Good morrow, neighbor Baptista.

Bap. Good morrow, neighbor Gremio. God save
    you, gentlemen! 45

Pet. And you, good sir. Pray, have you not a
    daughter

Called Katherina, fair and virtuous?

Bap. I have a daughter, sir, called Katherina.

Gre. You are too blunt; go to it orderly. 50

Pet. You wrong me, Signior Gremio; give me
    leave.

I am a gentleman of Verona, sir,

That, hearing of her beauty and her wit,

Her affability and bashful modesty, 55

Her wondrous qualities and mild behavior,

Am bold to show myself a forward guest

Within your house, to make mine eye the witness

Of that report which I so oft have heard.

And, for an entrance to my entertainment, 60

I do present you with a man of mine,

                [Presenting Hortensio]

Cunning in music and the mathematics,

To instruct her fully in those sciences,

Whereof I know she is not ignorant.

Accept of him, or else you do me wrong: 65

79. **Saving your tale:** an apology for interrupting his speech.

81. **Bacare:** a pseudo-Latin cant word: "back with you! down boy!"

His name is Licio, born in Mantua.

   Bap. Y'are welcome, sir; and he, for your good
    sake.

But for my daughter Katherine, this I know,

She is not for your turn, the more my grief.   70

   Pet. I see you do not mean to part with her,

Or else you like not of my company.

   Bap. Mistake me not; I speak but as I find.

Whence are you, sir? What may I call your name?

   Pet. Petruchio is my name, Antonio's son,   75

A man well known throughout all Italy.

   Bap. I know him well; you are welcome for his
    sake.

   Gre. Saving your tale, Petruchio, I pray,

Let us, that are poor petitioners, speak too.   80

Bacare! you are marvelous forward.

   Pet. O, pardon me, Signior Gremio, I would fain
    be doing.

   Gre. I doubt it not, sir; but you will curse your
    wooing.   85

Neighbor, this is a gift very grateful, I am sure of
it. To express the like kindness, myself, that have
been more kindly beholding to you than any, freely
give unto you this young scholar, [*Presenting Lucentio*] that hath been long studying at Rheims; as 90
cunning in Greek, Latin, and other languages, as the
other in music and mathematics. His name is Cambio; pray accept his service.

   Bap. A thousand thanks, Signior Gremio. Wel-

103. preferment of: giving precedence to.

come, good Cambio. [*To Tranio*] But, gentle sir,   95
methinks you walk like a stranger; may I be so bold
to know the cause of your coming?
   Tra./Luc. Pardon me, sir, the boldness is mine own,
That, being a stranger in this city here,
Do make myself a suitor to your daughter,   100
Unto Bianca, fair and virtuous.
Nor is your firm resolve unknown to me
In the preferment of the eldest sister.
This liberty is all that I request,
That, upon knowledge of my parentage,   105
I may have welcome 'mongst the rest that woo,
And free access and favor as the rest.
And, toward the education of your daughters,
I here bestow a simple instrument,
And this small packet of Greek and Latin books: 110
If you accept them, then their worth is great.
   Bap. Lucentio is your name, of whence, I pray?
   Tra./Luc. Of Pisa, sir; son to Vincentio.
   Bap. A mighty man of Pisa; by report
I know him well. You are very welcome, sir.   115
[*To Hortensio*] Take you that lute, [*To Lucentio*]
   and you the set of books;
You shall go see your pupils presently.
Holla, within!

Enter a Servant.

       Sirrah, lead these gentlemen   120
To my daughters, and tell them both

123. **orchard:** formal garden.

127. **every day I cannot come to woo:** a line from the refrain of an old song.

136. **widowhood:** widow's share in her husband's estate.

138. **specialties:** precise terms of contract.

These are their tutors: bid them use them well.
          [*Exit Servant, with Lucentio and*
                Hortensio, Biondello following.]
We will go walk a little in the orchard
And then to dinner. You are passing welcome,
And so I pray you all to think yourselves.   125

Pet. Signior Baptista, my business asketh haste,
And every day I cannot come to woo.
You knew my father well, and in him me,
Left solely heir to all his lands and goods,
Which I have bettered rather than decreased: 130
Then tell me, if I get your daughter's love,
What dowry shall I have with her to wife?

Bap. After my death the one half of my lands,
And in possession twenty thousand crowns.

Pet. And, for that dowry, I'll assure her of   135
Her widowhood, be it that she survive me,
In all my lands and leases whatsoever.
Let specialties be therefore drawn between us
That covenants may be kept on either hand.

Bap. Ay, when the special thing is well obtained,   140
That is, her love; for that is all in all.

Pet. Why, that is nothing; for I tell you, father,
I am as peremptory as she proud-minded;
And where two raging fires meet together
They do consume the thing that feeds their fury: 145
Though little fire grows great with little wind,
Yet extreme gusts will blow out fire and all;
So I to her, and so she yields to me;
For I am rough and woo not like a babe.

150. **speed:** progress; luck.

152. **proof:** utmost trial.

165. **mistook her frets:** i.e., her fingering was faulty. The **frets** of a stringed instrument are guides to fingering.

168. **Frets . . . I'll fume:** cf. the phrase "To fret and fume."

172. **amazed:** stunned.

176. **As had she:** as if she had.

Bap. Well mayst thou woo and happy be thy speed!   150
But be thou armed for some unhappy words.
   Pet. Ay, to the proof; as mountains are for winds,
That shake not, though they blow perpetually.

Enter Hortensio [(Licio)], with his head broke.

   Bap. How now, my friend! Why dost thou look
      so pale?   155
   Hor./Lic. For fear, I promise you, if I look pale.
   Bap. What, will my daughter prove a good mu-
      sician?
   Hor./Lic. I think she'll sooner prove a soldier.
Iron may hold with her but never lutes.   160
   Bap. Why, then, thou canst not break her to the
      lute?
   Hor./Lic. Why, no; for she hath broke the lute to
      me.
I did but tell her she mistook her frets   165
And bowed her hand to teach her fingering;
When, with a most impatient devilish spirit,
"Frets, call you these?" quoth she; "I'll fume with
      them";
And, with that word, she struck me on the head,   170
And through the instrument my pate made way.
And there I stood amazed for a while
As on a pillory, looking through the lute,
While she did call me rascal, fiddler,
And twangling Jack, with twenty such vile terms   175
As had she studied to misuse me so.

177. **lusty:** spirited.
183. **apt to learn:** responsive to instruction.
186. **attend:** await.
195. **pack:** pack myself off.
197. **deny:** refuse; **crave:** request.
198. **banes:** banns.

Pet. Now, by the world, it is a lusty wench!
I love her ten times more than e'er I did:
O, how I long to have some chat with her!
   Bap. [*To Hortensio*] Well, go with me, and be not 180
    so discomfited.
Proceed in practice with my younger daughter;
She's apt to learn and thankful for good turns.
Signior Petruchio, will you go with us,
Or shall I send my daughter Kate to you? 185
               Exeunt [*all but Petruchio*].
   Pet. I pray you do; I will attend her here
And woo her with some spirit when she comes.
Say that she rail, why then I'll tell her plain
She sings as sweetly as a nightingale;
Say that she frown, I'll say she looks as clear 190
As morning roses newly washed with dew;
Say she be mute and will not speak a word,
Then I'll commend her volubility,
And say she uttereth piercing eloquence.
If she do bid me pack, I'll give her thanks, 195
As though she bid me stay by her a week;
If she deny to wed, I'll crave the day
When I shall ask the banes, and when be married.
But here she comes; and now, Petruchio, speak.

         Enter Katherina.

Good morrow, Kate; for that's your name, I hear. 200
   Kat. Well have you heard, but something hard of
    hearing:

209. **dainties are all Kates:** a pun on the word "cates," meaning dainty tidbits.

212. **sounded:** (1) spoken of, (2) measured by "sounding."

218. **movable:** a movable piece of property; something replaceable.

227. **light:** lively; quickwitted; **swain:** rustic.

229. **buzz:** i.e., like a bee.

230. **buzzard:** secondary meaning is "a stupid person."

231. **turtle:** turtledove; **buzzard:** a predatory hawk, rather than a scavenging vulture.

They call me Katherina that do talk of me.

  Pet. You lie, in faith; for you are called plain Kate,   205
And bonny Kate, and sometimes Kate the curst;
But, Kate, the prettiest Kate in Christendom;
Kate of Kate-Hall, my superdainty Kate,
For dainties are all Kates: and therefore, Kate,
Take this of me, Kate of my consolation: 210
Hearing thy mildness praised in every town,
Thy virtues spoke of, and thy beauty sounded—
Yet not so deeply as to thee belongs—
Myself am moved to woo thee for my wife.

  Kat. Moved! In good time: let him that moved 215
    you hither
Remove you hence. I knew you at the first
You were a movable.

  Pet.   Why, what's a movable?

  Kat. A joint stool.   220

  Pet.   Thou hast hit it: come sit on me.

  Kat. Asses are made to bear, and so are you.

  Pet. Women are made to bear, and so are you.

  Kat. No such jade as you, if me you mean.

  Pet. Alas, good Kate, I will not burden thee; 225
For, knowing thee to be but young and light—

  Kat. Too light for such a swain as you to catch,
And yet as heavy as my weight should be.

  Pet. Should be! should—buzz!

  Kat.   Well ta'en, and like a buzzard. 230

  Pet. O slow-winged turtle! shall a buzzard take
    thee?

233. **for a turtle, as he takes a buzzard:** i.e., for a meek defenseless creature, when I am really a match for him.

244. **talk of tales:** i.e., chat idly.

252. **if no gentleman, why then no arms:** only gentlemen were entitled to bear coats of arms.

253. **books:** heralds' books, in which coats of arms were recorded; cf. also the phrase "in one's good books" (favor).

259. **crab:** crab apple.

Kat. Ay, for a turtle, as he takes a buzzard.

Pet. Come, come, you wasp; i' faith you are too
   angry.   235

Kat. If I be waspish, best beware my sting.

Pet. My remedy is then to pluck it out.

Kat. Ay, if the fool could find it where it lies.

Pet. Who knows not where a wasp does wear his
   sting?   240
In his tail.

Kat. In his tongue.

Pet.   Whose tongue?

Kat. Yours, if you talk of tales; and so farewell.

Pet. What! with my tongue in your tail? Nay, come 245
   again.
Good Kate, I am a gentleman.

Kat.   That I'll try.

                              She strikes him.

Pet. I swear I'll cuff you, if you strike again.

Kat. So may you lose your arms: 250
If you strike me, you are no gentleman,
And if no gentleman, why then no arms.

Pet. A herald, Kate? O, put me in thy books!

Kat. What is your crest? a coxcomb?

Pet. A combless cock, so Kate will be my hen.   255

Kat. No cock of mine; you crow too like a craven.

Pet. Nay, come, Kate, come; you must not look
   so sour.

Kat. It is my fashion when I see a crab.

Pet. Why, here's no crab, and therefore look not 260
   sour.

266. **aimed:** guessed; **of:** by.
275. **coy:** disdainful.
276. **very:** downright.
283. **conference:** conversation.
289. **whom thou keepst command:** i.e., keep your orders for your servants.

Kat. There is, there is.

Pet. Then show it me.

Kat.   Had I a glass I would.

Pet. What, you mean my face? 265

Kat.   Well aimed of such a young one.

Pet. Now, by Saint George, I am too young for you.

Kat. Yet you are withered.

Pet.   'Tis with cares.

Kat.   I care not. 270

Pet. Nay, hear you, Kate; in sooth you scape not
so.

Kat. I chafe you if I tarry; let me go.

Pet. No, not a whit; I find you passing gentle.
'Twas told me you were rough and coy and sullen, 275
And now I find report a very liar;
For thou art pleasant, gamesome, passing courteous,
But slow in speech, yet sweet as springtime flowers.
Thou canst not frown, thou canst not look askance,
Nor bite the lip as angry wenches will, 280
Nor hast thou pleasure to be cross in talk;
But thou with mildness entertainst thy wooers,
With gentle conference, soft and affable.
Why does the world report that Kate doth limp?
O sland'rous world! Kate, like the hazel twig 285
Is straight and slender, and as brown in hue
As hazelnuts and sweeter than the kernels.
O, let me see thee walk: thou dost not halt!

Kat. Go, fool, and whom thou keepst command.

Pet. Did ever Dian so become a grove 290
As Kate this chamber with her princely gait?

298. **keep you warm:** a reference to a proverbial idea that even a fool has enough wit to keep himself warm (or dry).

303. **will you, nill you:** willy-nilly; whether you will or not.

O, be thou Dian and let her be Kate,
And then let Kate be chaste and Dian sportful!
   Kat. Where did you study all this goodly speech?
   Pet. It is extempore, from my mother wit.   295
   Kat. A witty mother! witless else her son.
   Pet. Am I not wise?
   Kat.   Yes; keep you warm.
   Pet. Marry, so I mean, sweet Katherine, in thy bed;
And therefore, setting all this chat aside,   300
Thus in plain terms: your father hath consented
That you shall be my wife, your dowry 'greed on;
And will you, nill you, I will marry you.
Now, Kate, I am a husband for your turn;
For, by this light, whereby I see thy beauty—   305
Thy beauty that doth make me like thee well—
Thou must be married to no man but me.

Enter Baptista, Gremio, [and] Tranio [(Lucentio)].

For I am he am born to tame you, Kate,
And bring you from a wild Kate to a Kate
Conformable as other household Kates.   310
Here comes your father: never make denial;
I must and will have Katherine to my wife.
   Bap. Now, Signior Petruchio, how speed you with
    my daughter?
   Pet. How but well, sir? how but well?   315
It were impossible I should speed amiss.
   Bap. Why, how now, daughter Katherine! in your
    dumps?

319. **promise:** assure.

323. **Jack:** knave; presumptuous fellow.

327. **for policy:** deliberately.

330. **Grissel:** the Patient Griselda of Boccaccio's tale in the *Decameron,* whose loyal obedience to her husband became legendary.

331. **Lucrece:** the Roman matron who killed herself for shame after being raped by Tarquin (the subject of Shakespeare's poem *The Rape of Lucrece*).

343. **still:** always.

347. **vied:** offered repeatedly.

Kat. Call you me daughter? Now, I promise
    you,   320
You have showed a tender fatherly regard
To wish me wed to one half lunatic,
A madcap ruffian and a swearing Jack,
That thinks with oaths to face the matter out.

Pet. Father, 'tis thus: yourself and all the world 325
That talked of her have talked amiss of her.
If she be curst, it is for policy,
For she's not froward but modest as the dove;
She is not hot but temperate as the morn;
For patience she will prove a second Grissel,   330
And Roman Lucrece for her chastity;
And to conclude, we have 'greed so well together
That upon Sunday is the wedding day.

Kat. I'll see thee hanged on Sunday first.

Gre. Hark, Petruchio: she says she'll see thee 335
    hanged first.

Tra./Luc. Is this your speeding? Nay, then good
    night our part!

Pet. Be patient, gentlemen, I choose her for my-
    self;   340
If she and I be pleased, what's that to you?
'Tis bargained 'twixt us twain, being alone,
That she shall still be curst in company.
I tell you, 'tis incredible to believe
How much she loves me. O, the kindest Kate!   345
She hung about my neck, and kiss on kiss
She vied so fast, protesting oath on oath,
That in a twink she won me to her love.

349. **world:** wonder; marvelous sight.

351. **meacock:** effeminate; cowardly.

353. **'gainst:** in preparation for.

354. **bid:** invite.

355. **fine:** finely clothed.

364. **a:** on.

365. **clapped up:** agreed upon (with handshakes to seal the bargain).

369. **fretting by you:** (1) vexing you (with reference to Katherina's temper), (2) wearing away (as cloth does in use).

O, you are novices! 'Tis a world to see
How tame, when men and women are alone,   350
A meacock wretch can make the curstest shrew.
Give me thy hand, Kate: I will unto Venice
To buy apparel 'gainst the wedding day.
Provide the feast, father, and bid the guests;
I will be sure my Katherine shall be fine.   355

    Bap. I know not what to say; but give me your
      hands.
God send you joy, Petruchio! 'tis a match.

    Gre., Tra./Luc. Amen, say we: we will be wit-
      nesses.   360

    Pet. Father, and wife, and gentlemen, adieu.
I will to Venice; Sunday comes apace.
We will have rings and things and fine array;
And, kiss me, Kate, we will be married a Sunday.

                Exeunt Petruchio and Katherine.

    Gre. Was ever match clapped up so suddenly?   365

    Bap. Faith, gentlemen, now I play a merchant's
      part
And venture madly on a desperate mart.

    Tra./Luc. 'Twas a commodity lay fretting by you;
'Twill bring you gain or perish on the seas.   370

    Bap. The gain I seek is quiet in the match.

    Gre. No doubt but he hath got a quiet catch.
But now, Baptista, to your younger daughter:
Now is the day we long have looked for;
I am your neighbor, and was suitor first.   375

    Tra./Luc. And I am one that love Bianca more
Than words can witness or your thoughts can guess.

381. **Skipper:** a contemptuous epithet for a frivolous youth, an upstart.

383. **compound:** settle.

385. **both:** i.e., the two suitors.

393. **Tyrian:** dark-red-colored; cf. Tyrian purple.

394. **crowns:** gold coins.

395. **arras counterpoints:** tapestry counterpanes. The word **arras** comes from the place of that name in France, where fine tapestries were produced.

397. **Turkey cushions:** cushions of embroidered or tufted fabric imitative of Turkish carpet; **bossed:** embroidered.

398. **Valance:** drapery borders, probably for counterpanes.

401. **milch kine to the pail:** cows giving milk.

403. **all things answerable to this portion:** i.e., everything else on the same scale as the property enumerated.

404. **struck:** advanced.

Gre. Youngling, thou canst not love so dear as I.

Tra./Luc. Greybeard, thy love doth freeze.

Gre.   But thine doth fry.   380

Skipper, stand back, 'tis age that nourisheth.

Tra./Luc. But youth in ladies' eyes that flourisheth.

Bap. Content you, gentlemen; I will compound this
strife:

'Tis deeds must win the prize, and he, of both,   385

That can assure my daughter greatest dower

Shall have my Bianca's love.

Say, Signior Gremio, what can you assure her?

Gre. First, as you know, my house within the
city   390

Is richly furnished with plate and gold:

Basins and ewers to lave her dainty hands;

My hangings all of Tyrian tapestry;

In ivory coffers I have stuffed my crowns;

In cypress chests my arras counterpoints,   395

Costly apparel, tents, and canopies.

Fine linen, Turkey cushions bossed with pearl,

Valance of Venice gold in needlework,

Pewter and brass, and all things that belong

To house or housekeeping. Then, at my farm   400

I have a hundred milch kine to the pail,

Sixscore fat oxen standing in my stalls,

And all things answerable to this portion.

Myself am struck in years, I must confess;

And if I die tomorrow, this is hers,   405

If whilst I live she will be only mine.

Tra./Luc. That "only" came well in. Sir, list to me:

414. **jointure:** portion of estate; marriage settlement.

418. **argosy:** large merchant vessel (derived from the port Ragusa, known as "Arragosa" in this period).

422. **galliasses:** vessels somewhat larger and heavier than galleys.

423. **tight:** sound; seaworthy.

432. **assurance:** guarantee.

I am my father's heir and only son;
If I may have your daughter to my wife
I'll leave her houses three or four as good,   410
Within rich Pisa walls, as any one
Old Signior Gremio has in Padua;
Besides two thousand ducats by the year
Of fruitful land, all which shall be her jointure.
What, have I pinched you, Signior Gremio?   415
   Gre. Two thousand ducats by the year of land!
My land amounts not to so much in all:
That she shall have, besides an argosy
That now is lying in Marseilles' road.
What, have I choked you with an argosy?   420
   Tra./Luc. Gremio, 'tis known my father hath no less
Than three great argosies, besides two galliasses
And twelve tight galleys; these I will assure her,
And twice as much, whate'er thou off'rest next.
   Gre. Nay, I have off'red all, I have no more;   425
And she can have no more than all I have.
If you like me, she shall have me and mine.
   Tra./Luc. Why, then the maid is mine from all the
    world
By your firm promise. Gremio is outvied.   430
   Bap. I must confess your offer is the best;
And, let your father make her the assurance,
She is your own; else, you must pardon me,
If you should die before him, where's her dower?
   Tra./Luc. That's but a cavil: he is old, I young. 435
   Gre. And may not young men die as well as old?
   Bap. Well, gentlemen,

445. **gamester:** i.e., one who is gambling on his father's acquiescence.

447. **Set foot under thy table:** become your dependent; **toy:** piece of nonsense.

451. **faced it with a card of ten:** bluffed with a low card.

I am thus resolved. On Sunday next, you know,
My daughter Katherine is to be married:
Now, on the Sunday following, shall Bianca   440
Be bride to you if you make this assurance;
If not, to Signior Gremio:
And so I take my leave and thank you both.   *Exit.*

  Gre. Adieu, good neighbor. Now I fear thee not:
Sirrah young gamester, your father were a fool   445
To give thee all and in his waning age
Set foot under thy table. Tut! a toy!
An old Italian fox is not so kind, my boy.   *Exit.*

    Tra./Luc. A vengeance on your crafty withered
        hide!   450
Yet I have faced it with a card of ten.
'Tis in my head to do my master good:
I see no reason but supposed Lucentio
Must get a father, called "supposed Vincentio";
And that's a wonder: fathers commonly   455
Do get their children, but in this case of wooing,
A child shall get a sire, if I fail not of my cunning.
                                            Exit.

THE
TAMING OF
THE SHREW

ACT III

III. [i.] The rivals Cambio (Lucentio) and Licio (Hortensio) "instruct" Bianca. Under cover of teaching her Latin, Lucentio reveals his true identity to the girl and explains his motives. Hortensio uses the explanation of the gamut to reveal himself, but Bianca seems indifferent. Hortensio is already suspicious that Lucentio has amorous designs on Bianca and declares that he will give her up if her affections can incline to so lowly a creature as a schoolmaster.

||||||||||||||||||||||||||||||||||||

7. **prerogative:** privilege of precedence.

10. **Preposterous:** placing first that which should be last, because (according to Aristotle) study should precede music, which should be reserved for recreation.

15. **serve in:** present.

16. **braves:** challenges; presumptuous speeches.

20. **breeching scholar:** schoolboy subject to **breeching** (whipping by the master).

[ACT III]

[Scene I. Padua. Baptista's house.]

*Enter Lucentio [(Cambio)], Hortensio [(Licio)],
and Bianca.*

Luc./Cam. Fiddler, forbear; you grow too forward,
    sir.
Have you so soon forgot the entertainment
Her sister Katherine welcomed you withal?
    Hor./Lic. But, wrangling pedant, this is   5
The patroness of heavenly harmony.
Then give me leave to have prerogative;
And when in music we have spent an hour
Your lecture shall have leisure for as much.
    Luc./Cam. Preposterous ass, that never read so far 10
To know the cause why music was ordained!
Was it not to refresh the mind of man
After his studies or his usual pain?
Then give me leave to read philosophy,
And while I pause, serve in your harmony.   15
    Hor./Lic. Sirrah, I will not bear these braves of
    thine.
    Bia. Why, gentlemen, you do me double wrong
To strive for that which resteth in my choice.
I am no breeching scholar in the schools;   20

50

32–3. Hic ibat Simois; hic est Sigeia tellus;/ Hic steterat Priami regia celsa senis: "Here flowed the Simois; this is the Sigeian land;/Here stood the lofty palace of Priam the ancient" (Ovid, *Heroides,* i.33–4). According to Homer, most of the battles of the Trojan war were fought near the town of Sigaeum or Sigeum.

34. Conster: construe; translate.

39. bearing my port: assuming my social position.

43. Spit in the hole: "try again with renewed vigor." The reference is to spitting on the hands before applying oneself to a task for the second time; the action of spitting in the lute would hinder rather than help its tuning.

Greek heroes at Troy. From Ovid, *Metamorphoses* (1522).

I'll not be tied to hours nor 'pointed times,
But learn my lessons as I please myself.
And, to cut off all strife, here sit we down;
Take you your instrument, play you the whiles;
His lecture will be done ere you have tuned.   25

   Hor./Lic. You'll leave his lecture when I am in
    tune?

   Luc./Cam. That will be never; tune your instrument.

   Bia. Where left we last?   30

   Luc./Cam. Here, madam:
Hic ibat Simois; hic est Sigeia tellus;
Hic steterat Priami regia celsa senis.

   Bia. Conster them.

   Luc./Cam. Hic ibat, as I told you before, *Simois,* I 35
am Lucentio, *hic est,* son unto Vincentio of Pisa, *Si-*
geia tellus, disguised thus to get your love; *Hic*
steterat, and that Lucentio that comes a-wooing, *Pri-*
ami, is my man Tranio, *regia,* bearing my port, *celsa*
senis, that we might beguile the old pantaloon.   40

   Hor./Lic. Madam, my instrument's in tune.

   Bia. Let's hear.—O fie! the treble jars.

   Luc./Cam. Spit in the hole, man, and tune again.

   Bia. Now let me see if I can conster it: *Hic ibat*
Simois, I know you not, *hic est Sigeia tellus,* I trust 45
you not; *Hic steterat Priami,* take heed he hear us
not, *regia,* presume not, *celsa senis,* despair not.

   Hor./Lic. Madam, 'tis now in tune.

   Luc./Cam.   All but the bass.

54. **Pedascule:** pseudo-Latin, meaning "little pedant."

56. **Aeacides:** this name for the Greek hero Ajax appears in the next line following the passage from Ovid quoted in lines 32–3 above. Lucentio pretends that the construing of Latin has continued while Hortensio tuned the lute.

68. **but:** unless.

73. **gamut:** the model scale devised by Guido of Arezzo in the eleventh century. The scale was divided into groups of six sounds (hexachords), which were sung to the syllables *ut, re, mi, fa, sol, la,* while the notes were known as *A, B, C, D, E, F,* and *G* (gamma).

 Hor./Lic. The bass is right; 'tis the base knave   50
  that jars.
[*Aside*] How fiery and forward our pedant is!
Now, for my life, the knave doth court my love;
Pedascule, I'll watch you better yet.
 Bia. In time I may believe, yet I mistrust.   55
 Luc./Cam. Mistrust it not; for, sure, Aeacides
Was Ajax, called so from his grandfather.
 Bia. I must believe my master; else, I promise you,
I should be arguing still upon that doubt;
But let it rest. Now, Licio, to you.   60
Good master, take it not unkindly, pray,
That I have been thus pleasant with you both.
 Hor./Lic. You may go walk and give me leave a
  while;
My lessons make no music in three parts.   65
 Luc./Cam. Are you so formal, sir? [*Aside*] Well, I
  must wait
And watch withal; for, but I be deceived,
Our fine musician groweth amorous.
 Hor./Lic. Madam, before you touch the instrument   70
To learn the order of my fingering,
I must begin with rudiments of art
To teach you gamut in a briefer sort,
More pleasant, pithy, and effectual,
Than hath been taught by any of my trade;   75
And there it is in writing, fairly drawn.
 Bia. Why, I am past my gamut long ago.
 Hor./Lic. Yet read the gamut of Hortensio.

79. **ground:** lowest note; basis; **accord:** harmony.

86. **nice:** whimsical.

87. **To:** as to.

99. **stale:** decoy.

100. **Seize thee that list:** whoever wants thee may have thee; **ranging:** straying. The imagery is that of an untrained falcon that fails to pursue proper game.

101. **be quit with:** have done with.

Bia. "'Gamut' I am, the ground of all accord,
     A re, to plead Hortensio's passion;   80
   B mi, Bianca, take him for thy lord,
     C fa ut, that loves with all affection;
     D sol re, one clef, two notes have I;
     E la mi, show pity or I die."
Call you this gamut? Tut, I like it not.   85
Old fashions please me best; I am not so nice
To change true rules for odd inventions.

Enter a Messenger.

  Mess. Mistress, your father prays you leave your
    books
And help to dress your sister's chamber up;   90
You know tomorrow is the wedding day.
  Bia. Farewell, sweet masters both; I must be
    gone.   *[Exeunt Bianca and Messenger.]*
  Luc./Cam. Faith, mistress, then I have no cause
    to stay.   *[Exit.]*   95
  Hor./Lic. But I have cause to pry into this pedant.
Methinks he looks as though he were in love.
Yet if thy thoughts, Bianca, be so humble
To cast thy wand'ring eyes on every stale,
Seize thee that list; if once I find thee ranging,   100
Hortensio will be quit with thee by changing.
                            Exit.

III. **[ii.]** On the appointed day for the wedding of Katherina and Petruchio, the bridegroom is slow in arriving, and Katherina is humiliated at his apparent desertion. When Petruchio arrives, everyone is shocked at the absurdity of his dress and behavior. He resists all urging to change to more suitable attire and continues his antic behavior throughout the wedding ceremony. Immediately after the ceremony, Petruchio announces that they must be off at once, and he will listen to no entreaty to stay for the customary wedding dinner. Katherina begs, then storms; but Petruchio, pretending that the company threatens her safety, forcibly carries her off.

6. **want:** lack.

9. **forsooth:** indeed.

12. **rudesby:** boor; barbarian; **spleen:** capricious impulse.

14. **frantic:** mad.

16. **noted for:** known as.

[Scene II. Padua. Before Baptista's house.]

Enter Baptista, Gremio, Tranio [(Lucentio)],
Katherina, Bianca, [Lucentio (Cambio),] and
others; Attendants.

Bap. [*To Tranio*] Signior Lucentio, this is the
'pointed day
That Katherine and Petruchio should be married,
And yet we hear not of our son-in-law.
What will be said? What mockery will it be   5
To want the bridegroom when the priest attends
To speak the ceremonial rites of marriage!
What says Lucentio to this shame of ours?
Kat. No shame but mine; I must, forsooth, be
forced   10
To give my hand opposed against my heart
Unto a mad-brain rudesby, full of spleen,
Who wooed in haste and means to wed at leisure.
I told you, I, he was a frantic fool,
Hiding his bitter jests in blunt behavior;   15
And to be noted for a merry man,
He'll woo a thousand, 'point the day of marriage,
Make friends, invite, and proclaim the banes;
Yet never means to wed where he hath wooed.
Now must the world point at poor Katherine   20
And say, "Lo! there is mad Petruchio's wife,
If it would please him come and marry her."
Tra./Luc. Patience, good Katherine, and Baptista
too.

33. [**old news!**]: added by the editor Edward Capell. Note that the word **old** ("extraordinary") is necessary to warrant the play on the word in the next line.

50. **chapeless:** lacking the metal tip to the sheath.

51. **points:** laces (so that his hose and breeches have parted company in two places); **hipped:** lame-hipped.

SPOSA DI PADOVA,

A bride of Padua. From Cesare Vecellio, *De gli habiti antichi et moderni* (1590).

Upon my life, Petruchio means but well,   25
Whatever fortune stays him from his word.
Though he be blunt, I know him passing wise;
Though he be merry, yet withal he's honest.
　Kat. Would Katherine had never seen him though!
　　Exit weeping [followed by Bianca and others].
　Bap. Go, girl: I cannot blame thee now to weep,   30
For such an injury would vex a very saint,
Much more a shrew of thy impatient humor.

                Enter Biondello.

　Bio. Master, master! news! [old news!] and such
news as you never heard of!
　Bap. Is it new and old too? How may that be?   35
　Bio. Why, is it not news to hear of Petruchio's
coming?
　Bap. Is he come?
　Bio. Why, no, sir.
　Bap. What then?   40
　Bio. He is coming.
　Bap. When will he be here?
　Bio. When he stands where I am and sees you
there.
　Tra./Luc. But, say, what to thine old news?   45
　Bio. Why, Petruchio is coming, in a new hat and
an old jerkin; a pair of old breeches thrice turned; a
pair of boots that have been candle cases, one buck-
led, another laced; an old rusty sword ta'en out of
the town armory, with a broken hilt, and chapeless;   50
with two broken points: his horse hipped with an old

52. **mothy:** motheaten; **of no kindred:** un-matched.

53–4. **glanders:** swellings under the jaw; **like to mose in the chine:** "mourning of the chine" was a term for a horse ailment similar to glanders. *Webster's Second International Dictionary* explains this phrase as a "corruption of *mortersheen,* glanders, apparently influenced by the dialect word *mose,* to mold, rot."

54–5. **lampass:** an infection causing swellings in the mouth that interfered with the ability to eat; **the fashions:** a corruption of "farcy," a disease akin to glanders characterized by swellings on the lymph glands; **windgalls:** tumors on the fetlock joints; **spavins:** bony tumors on the hock of the leg; **rayed:** berayed (befouled).

56. **fives:** dialect form of "vives": hard swellings of the submaxillary glands.

57. **staggers:** a disease affecting the brain and spinal cord, causing staggering and reeling; **bots:** intestinal parasites.

58. **shoulder-shotten:** having a shoulder out of joint; **near-legged before:** having front legs so close that the forefeet knock together.

59. **half-checked bit:** the sidepieces of a bit are known as "checks" or "cheeks." Gervase Markham, *Cavelarice; or, The English Horseman* (1607), advised that "the more compass a bit carrieth, the more it compasseth and bringeth in the horse's head, and the straiter the cheek is, the more it putteth up and advanceth both the head, neck, and muzzle." Petru-

(Continued on next page)

mothy saddle and stirrups of no kindred; besides,
possessed with the glanders and like to mose in the
chine; troubled with the lampass, infected with the
fashions, full of windgalls, sped with spavins, rayed   55
with the yellows, past cure of the fives, stark spoiled
with the staggers, begnawn with the bots, swayed in
the back, and shoulder-shotten; near-legged before,
and with a half-checked bit, and a headstall of sheep's
leather, which, being restrained to keep him from   60
stumbling, hath been often burst and now repaired
with knots; one girth six times pieced, and a woman's
crupper of velure, which hath two letters for her
name fairly set down in studs, and here and there
pieced with packthread.   65

Bap. Who comes with him?

Bio. O, sir! his lackey, for all the world caparisoned
like the horse; with a linen stock on one leg and a
kersey boothose on the other, gart'red with a red and
blue list; an old hat, and the humor of forty fancies   70
pricked in't for a feather: a monster, a very monster
in apparel, and not like a Christian footboy or a gentleman's lackey.

Tra./Luc. 'Tis some odd humor pricks him to this
     fashion,   75
Yet oftentimes he goes but mean appareled.

Bap. I am glad he's come, howsoe'er he comes.

Bio. Why, sir, he comes not.

Bap. Didst thou not say he comes?

Bio. Who? that Petruchio came?   80

Bap. Ay, that Petruchio came.

(*Continued from Page 56*)
chio's horse is inadequately controlled so that his head is allowed to droop, adding to his unsightly appearance; **headstall:** the part of a bridle that goes over the head.

63. **velure:** a kind of velvet.

67. **caparisoned:** ornamented; bedecked.

68. **stock:** stocking.

69. **kersey:** coarse homespun woolen; **boothose:** heavy stockings worn under boots or in place of them to protect hose of a better quality.

70–1. **list:** strip of border of cloth; selvage; **the humor of forty fancies pricked in't:** probably, gaudily decorated in a ridiculous fashion.

86. **hold:** wager.

94. **halt:** limp.

99. **Gentles:** gentlemen.

102. **prodigy:** marvel.

107. **solemn:** ceremonious (not grave).

Varieties of "cheeks." From Gervase Markham, *Cavelarice; or, The English Horseman* (1607).

57

Bio. No, sir; I say his horse comes, with him on his
back.

Bap. Why, that's all one.

Bio. Nay, by Saint Jamy,   85
I hold you a penny,
A horse and a man
Is more than one,
And yet not many.

Enter Petruchio and Grumio.

Pet. Come, where be these gallants? Who is at   90
home?

Bap. You are welcome, sir.

Pet.   And yet I come not well.

Bap. And yet you halt not.

Tra./Luc.   Not so well appareled   95
As I wish you were.

Pet. Were it better I should rush in thus?
But where is Kate? Where is my lovely bride?
How does my father? Gentles, methinks you frown.
And wherefore gaze this goodly company   100
As if they saw some wondrous monument,
Some comet, or unusual prodigy?

Bap. Why, sir, you know this is your wedding day.
First were we sad, fearing you would not come;
Now sadder that you come so unprovided.   105
Fie! doff this habit, shame to your estate,
An eyesore to our solemn festival.

Tra./Luc. And tell us what occasion of import

113. **digress:** deviate from his promise.
118. **unreverent:** undignified.
123. **Good sooth:** in veritable truth.
131. **lovely:** loving.
135. **event:** outcome.
136. **But to her love:** the abruptness of Tranio's change of subject is probably to be accounted for by the loss of some lines here.

Hath all so long detained you from your wife
And sent you hither so unlike yourself?   110
   Pet. Tedious it were to tell and harsh to hear.
Sufficeth I am come to keep my word,
Though in some part enforced to digress;
Which, at more leisure, I will so excuse
As you shall well be satisfied with all.   115
But where is Kate? I stay too long from her;
The morning wears, 'tis time we were at church.
   Tra./Luc. See not your bride in these unreverent
    robes.
Go to my chamber; put on clothes of mine.   120
   Pet. Not I, believe me; thus I'll visit her.
   Bap. But thus, I trust, you will not marry her.
   Pet. Good sooth, even thus; therefore ha' done with
    words:
To me she's married, not unto my clothes.   125
Could I repair what she will wear in me
As I can change these poor accouterments,
'Twere well for Kate and better for myself.
But what a fool am I to chat with you
When I should bid good morrow to my bride   130
And seal the title with a lovely kiss!
                  Exit [with Grumio].
   Tra./Luc. He hath some meaning in his mad attire.
We will persuade him, be it possible,
To put on better ere he go to church.
   Bap. I'll after him and see the event of this.   135
           Exit [with Gremio and Attendants].
   Tra./Luc. But to her love concerneth us to add

140. **skills:** matters.
148. **steal our marriage:** i.e., elope.
152. **vantage:** advantage.
154. **narrow-prying:** suspiciously watchful.
155. **quaint:** clever.
161. **groom:** i.e., as uncouth as a stableboy.

Her father's liking; which to bring to pass,
As I before imparted to your Worship,
I am to get a man—whate'er he be
It skills not much, we'll fit him to our turn— 140
And he shall be Vincentio of Pisa,
And make assurance here in Padua
Of greater sums than I have promised.
So shall you quietly enjoy your hope,
And marry sweet Bianca with consent. 145
    Luc./Cam. Were it not that my fellow schoolmaster
Doth watch Bianca's steps so narrowly,
'Twere good, methinks, to steal our marriage;
Which once performed, let all the world say no,
I'll keep mine own despite of all the world. 150
    Tra./Luc. That by degrees we mean to look into,
And watch our vantage in this business;
We'll overreach the greybeard, Gremio,
The narrow-prying father, Minola,
The quaint musician, amorous Licio; 155
All for my master's sake, Lucentio.

Enter Gremio.

Signior Gremio, came you from the church?
    Gre. As willingly as e'er I came from school.
    Tra./Luc. And is the bride and bridegroom coming
        home? 160
    Gre. A bridegroom say you? 'Tis a groom indeed,
A grumbling groom, and that the girl shall find.
    Tra./Luc. Curster than she? Why, 'tis impossible.

166. **dam:** mother.

169. **Should . . . should:** must needs . . . would.

170. **gogs wouns:** a corruption of "by God's wounds."

175. **list:** desire.

178. **forwhy:** because.

180. **cozen:** cheat; i.e., Petruchio pretended that the interruption of the ceremony was deliberate on the priest's part.

184. **muscatel:** a sweet wine. It was customary for a cup of **muscatel** to be drunk by each member of the bridal party in turn at the end of the ceremony.

185. **sops:** morsels of cake floated in the wine.

187. **hungerly:** sparsely.

193. **rout:** company.

  Gre. Why, he's a devil, a devil, a very fiend.

  Tra./Luc. Why, she's a devil, a devil, the devil's 165
    dam.

  Gre. Tut! she's a lamb, a dove, a fool to him.
I'll tell you, Sir Lucentio: when the priest
Should ask if Katherine should be his wife,
"Ay, by gogs wouns!" quoth he; and swore so loud 170
That, all amazed, the priest let fall the book,
And, as he stooped again to take it up,
This mad-brained bridegroom took him such a cuff
That down fell priest and book and book and priest.
"Now, take them up," quoth he, "if any list." 175

  Tra./Luc. What said the wench when he rose
    again?

  Gre. Trembled and shook; forwhy he stamped and
    swore,
As if the vicar meant to cozen him. 180
But after many ceremonies done,
He calls for wine: "A health!" quoth he, as if
He had been aboard, carousing to his mates
After a storm; quaffed off the muscatel
And threw the sops all in the sexton's face, 185
Having no other reason
But that his beard grew thin and hungerly,
And seemed to ask him sops as he was drinking.
This done, he took the bride about the neck
And kissed her lips with such a clamorous smack 190
That at the parting all the church did echo,
And I, seeing this, came thence for very shame;
And after me, I know, the rout is coming.

Such a mad marriage never was before.
Hark, hark! I hear the minstrels play.   *Music plays.* 195

    Enter Petruchio, Katherina, Bianca, Baptista,
    Hortensio [(*Licio*) *with Grumio and Train*].

  Pet. Gentlemen and friends, I thank you for your
    pains.
I know you think to dine with me today
And have prepared great store of wedding cheer,
But so it is, my haste doth call me hence,   200
And therefore here I mean to take my leave.
  Bap. Is't possible you will away tonight?
  Pet. I must away today, before night come.
Make it no wonder; if you knew my business,
You would entreat me rather go than stay.   205
And, honest company, I thank you all,
That have beheld me give away myself
To this most patient, sweet, and virtuous wife.
Dine with my father, drink a health to me,
For I must hence; and farewell to you all.   210
  Tra./Luc. Let us entreat you stay till after dinner.
  Pet. It may not be.
  Gre.   Let me entreat you.
  Pet. It cannot be.
  Kat.   Let me entreat you.   215
  Pet. I am content.
  Kat.   Are you content to stay?
  Pet. I am content you shall entreat me stay,
But yet not stay, entreat me how you can.

222–23. they be ready; the oats have eaten the horses: i.e., it's time the horses were exercised; they have already overeaten.

228. whiles your boots are green: a proverbial expression urging a prompt departure to an unwanted guest. Cf. the modern phrase "Here's your hat, what's your hurry?"

230. jolly: arrogant.

231. take it on you: i.e., behave; **roundly:** undisguisedly; frankly.

233. what hast thou to do: what have you to say about it?

234. stay my leisure: await my pleasure in going.

241. domineer: synonymous with **revel** and **carouse.**

245. big: defiant; menacing. Petruchio addresses the company, which he pretends is threatening to take his wife from him; he ignores the fact that she herself is looking **big** at not having her own way.

Kat. Now, if you love me, stay.   220
Pet.   Grumio, my horse!
Gru. Ay, sir, they be ready; the oats have eaten the
horses.
Kat. Nay then,
Do what thou canst, I will not go today;   225
No, nor tomorrow, not till I please myself.
The door is open, sir, there lies your way;
You may be jogging whiles your boots are green;
For me, I'll not be gone till I please myself.
'Tis like you'll prove a jolly surly groom,   230
That take it on you at the first so roundly.
Pet. O Kate! content thee; prithee, be not angry.
Kat. I will be angry; what hast thou to do?
Father, be quiet; he shall stay my leisure.
Gre. Ay, marry, sir, now it begins to work.   235
Kat. Gentlemen, forward to the bridal dinner:
I see a woman may be made a fool
If she had not a spirit to resist.
Pet. They shall go forward, Kate, at thy command.
Obey the bride, you that attend on her;   240
Go to the feast, revel and domineer,
Carouse full measure to her maidenhead,
Be mad and merry, or go hang yourselves;
But for my bonny Kate, she must with me.
Nay, look not big, nor stamp, nor stare, nor fret;   245
I will be master of what is mine own.
She is my goods, my chattels; she is my house,
My household stuff, my field, my barn,
My horse, my ox, my ass, my anything;

257. **buckler thee:** act as thy shield.

265. **warrant:** guarantee; **Kated:** i.e., he has caught Kate's bad temper like an infectious disease.

267. **wants:** are lacking.

269. **junkets:** sweetmeats.

And here she stands, touch her whoever dare;   250
I'll bring mine action on the proudest he
That stops my way in Padua. Grumio,
Draw forth thy weapon, we are beset with thieves;
Rescue thy mistress, if thou be a man.

Fear not, sweet wench; they shall not touch thee,   255
    Kate:
I'll buckler thee against a million.

   Exeunt Petruchio, Katherina [and Grumio].

 Bap. Nay, let them go, a couple of quiet ones.
 Gre. Went they not quickly, I should die with
  laughing.   260
 Tra./Luc. Of all mad matches never was the like.
 Luc./Cam. Mistress, what's your opinion of your
  sister?
 Bia. That being mad herself, she's madly mated.
 Gre. I warrant him, Petruchio is Kated.   265
 Bap. Neighbors and friends, though bride and
  bridegroom wants
For to supply the places at the table,
You know there wants no junkets at the feast.
Lucentio, you shall supply the bridegroom's place,   270
And let Bianca take her sister's room.
 Tra./Luc. Shall sweet Bianca practice how to bride
  it?
 Bap. She shall, Lucentio. Come, gentlemen, let's go.
         Exeunt.

THE
TAMING OF
THE SHREW

ACT IV

[**IV. i.**] Grumio describes to Petruchio's other household servants the misadventures of his master and new mistress on the way home from the wedding. Katherina's horse fell on her in the mud and Petruchio used the accident as a pretext to assault Grumio, so that Katherina became further muddied in separating the two men. When the travel-weary couple arrive, Petruchio continues his role of unreasonable brute, finding fault with everything the servants do. He spurns the food prepared as unfit to eat and decrees that they will go supperless to bed rather than eat food that would make them choleric. Katherina's wedding night is to be spent listening to a lecture on continence from her new husband. Petruchio's plan is to tame his wife in the same manner as falcons are trained: by starvation and lack of sleep.

‖‖‖‖‖‖‖‖‖‖‖‖‖‖‖‖‖‖‖‖‖‖‖‖‖‖‖

2. **foul ways:** muddy roads.

3. **rayed:** fouled; see III.[ii.] 55.

5–6. **a little pot and soon hot:** proverbial. The literal meaning is that Grumio, like all small persons, has a hasty temper.

15. **run:** i.e., he compares his head and neck to a toboggan slide.

[ACT IV]

[Scene I. Petruchio's country house.]

Enter Grumio.

Gru. Fie, fie, on all tired jades, on all mad masters, and all foul ways! Was ever man so beaten? Was ever man so rayed? Was ever man so weary? I am sent before to make a fire, and they are coming after to warm them. Now were not I a little pot and soon 5 hot, my very lips might freeze to my teeth, my tongue to the roof of my mouth, my heart in my belly, ere I should come by a fire to thaw me; but I, with blowing the fire, shall warm myself; for, considering the weather, a taller man than I will take cold. Holla, ho! 10 Curtis.

Enter Curtis.

Cur. Who is that calls so coldly?

Gru. A piece of ice; if thou doubt it, thou mayst slide from my shoulder to my heel with no greater a run but my head and my neck. A fire, good Curtis. 15

Cur. Is my master and his wife coming, Grumio?

Gru. O, ay, Curtis, ay; and therefore fire, fire; cast on no water.

Cur. Is she so hot a shrew as she's reported?

25. **horn:** probably the **horn** of a cuckold (wronged husband). The accusation of having been cuckolded was a stock joke and might be offered to any man, married or single.

30. **hot office:** duty of providing heat.

34. **duty:** the reward earned by performance of his duty; the expression is apparently a proverbial one.

39. **"Jack, boy! ho, boy":** a snatch from a song, which goes on "The cat is in the well."

41. **cony-catching:** roguish tricks. Contemporary swindlers were known as "cony-catchers."

44. **trimmed:** neatened; put to rights.

45. **fustian:** a cotton fabric.

46. **officer:** servant.

47. **jacks:** (1) maleservants, (2) leather drinking vessels; **jills:** (1) maidservants, (2) containers of smaller capacity than **jacks; carpets:** commonly used as coverings for tables rather than as floor coverings.

Gru. She was, good Curtis, before this frost, but   20
thou knowest winter tames man, woman, and beast;
for it hath tamed my old master, and my new mistress, and myself, fellow Curtis.

Cur. Away, you three-inch fool! I am no beast.

Gru. Am I but three inches? Why, thy horn is a   25
foot; and so long am I at the least. But wilt thou
make a fire? or shall I complain on thee to our mistress, whose hand—she being now at hand—thou shalt
soon feel, to thy cold comfort, for being slow in thy
hot office.   30

Cur. I prithee, good Grumio, tell me, how goes the
world?

Gru. A cold world, Curtis, in every office but thine;
and therefore, fire. Do thy duty, and have thy duty,
for my master and mistress are almost frozen to   35
death.

Cur. There's fire ready; and therefore, good
Grumio, the news.

Gru. Why, "Jack, boy! ho, boy!" and as much news
as thou wilt.   40

Cur. Come, you are so full of cony-catching.

Gru. Why, therefore fire, for I have caught extreme cold. Where's the cook? Is supper ready, the
house trimmed, rushes strewed, cobwebs swept; the
servingmen in their new fustian, their white stock-   45
ings, and every officer his wedding garment on? Be
the jacks fair within, the jills fair without, the carpets
laid, and everything in order?

Cur. All ready; and therefore, I pray thee, news.

60. **sensible:** a secondary meaning is "able to be felt."

62. **Imprimis:** Latin, "first," commonly used for the first item of an inventory.

64. **of:** on.

70. **bemoiled:** muddied.

Gru. First, know, my horse is tired; my master and　50
mistress fall'n out.

Cur. How?

Gru. Out of their saddles into the dirt—and thereby
hangs a tale.

Cur. Let's ha't, good Grumio.　　　　　　　　　55

Gru. Lend thine ear.

Cur. Here.

Gru. There.　　　　　　　　　[*Strikes him.*]

Cur. This 'tis to feel a tale, not to hear a tale.

Gru. And therefore 'tis called a sensible tale, and　60
this cuff was but to knock at your ear and beseech
listening. Now I begin: *Imprimis,* we came down a
foul hill, my master riding behind my mistress—

Cur. Both of one horse?

Gru. What's that to thee?　　　　　　　　　65

Cur. Why, a horse.

Gru. Tell thou the tale; but hadst thou not crossed
me thou shouldst have heard how her horse fell, and
she under her horse; thou shouldst have heard in
how miry a place, how she was bemoiled: how he　70
left her with the horse upon her; how he beat me
because her horse stumbled; how she waded through
the dirt to pluck him off me; how he swore; how she
prayed, that never prayed before; how I cried; how
the horses ran away; how her bridle was burst; how　75
I lost my crupper; with many things of worthy mem-
ory, which now shall die in oblivion and thou return
unexperienced to thy grave.

Cur. By this reck'ning he is more shrew than she.

84. **blue coats:** blue, symbolizing loyalty, was a traditional color for servants' uniforms.

85. **indifferent:** conservative; inconspicuous.

92. **countenance:** show respect for.

97. **credit her:** do her respect.

Gru. Ay; and that thou and the proudest of you   80
all shall find when he comes home. But what talk I
of this? Call forth Nathaniel, Joseph, Nicholas, Philip,
Walter, Sugarsop, and the rest; let their heads be
slickly combed, their blue coats brushed and their
garters of an indifferent knit; let them curtsy with   85
their left legs and not presume to touch a hair of my
master's horsetail till they kiss their hands. Are they
all ready?

Cur. They are.

Gru. Call them forth.   90

Cur. Do you hear? ho! You must meet my master
to countenance my mistress.

Gru. Why, she hath a face of her own.

Cur. Who knows not that?

Gru. Thou, it seems, that calls for company to   95
countenance her.

Cur. I call them forth to credit her.

Gru. Why, she comes to borrow nothing of them.

Enter four or five Servingmen.

Nat. Welcome home, Grumio!

Phi. How now, Grumio!   100

Jos. What, Grumio!

Nic. Fellow Grumio!

Nat. How now, old lad!

Gru. Welcome, you; how now, you; what, you;
fellow, you; and thus much for greeting. Now, my   105
spruce companions, is all ready and all things neat?

Nat. All things is ready. How near is our master?

109. **Cock's:** a corruption of "God's."

116. **loggerheaded:** blockheaded.

120. **whoreson:** good-for-nothing; **malt-horse:** a heavy workhorse used in breweries, traditionally a type of clumsy and stupid worker.

125. **unpinked:** i.e., the ornamental punched (pinked) pattern is incomplete.

126. **link:** a small torch. Apparently, the black of the smoke from such torches was used like lampblack to refurbish faded black hats.

Gru. E'en at hand, alighted by this; and therefore
be not—Cock's passion, silence! I hear my master.

Enter Petruchio and Kate.

   Pet. Where be these knaves? What! no man at 110
    door
To hold my stirrup nor to take my horse?
Where is Nathaniel, Gregory, Philip?
   All Ser. Here, here, sir; here, sir.
   Pet. Here, sir! here, sir! here, sir! here, sir!   115
You loggerheaded and unpolished grooms!
What, no attendance? no regard? no duty?
Where is the foolish knave I sent before?
   Gru. Here, sir; as foolish as I was before.
   Pet. You peasant swain! you whoreson malt-horse 120
    drudge!
Did I not bid thee meet me in the park
And bring along these rascal knaves with thee?
   Gru. Nathaniel's coat, sir, was not fully made,
And Gabriel's pumps were all unpinked i' the heel;   125
There was no link to color Peter's hat,
And Walter's dagger was not come from sheathing;
There were none fine but Adam, Rafe, and Gregory;
The rest were ragged, old, and beggarly.
Yet, as they are, here are they come to meet you.   130
   Pet. Go, rascals, go, and fetch my supper in.
                             Exeunt Servants.
[*Sings*] "Where is the life that late I led?"
Where are those—? Sit down, Kate, and welcome.
Food, food, food, food!

135. **when:** "how long must I wait to be obeyed"?

144. **cousin Ferdinand:** this is the only mention of cousin Ferdinand, who never appears. George Steevens conjectured that he is mentioned "merely to show Katharina that he, like everything else, is at Petruchio's command."

152. **beetleheaded:** stupid. The **beetle** of the phrase is a wooden-headed mallet.

153. **stomach:** (1) appetite, (2) hasty temper.

Enter Servants with supper.

Why, when, I say?—Nay, good sweet Kate, be   135
     merry—
Off with my boots, you rogues! you villains! When?
[*Sings*] "It was the friar of orders grey,
As he forth walked on his way":
Out, you rogue! you pluck my foot awry;   140
Take that, and mend the plucking of the other.
                                        [*Strikes him.*]
Be merry, Kate. Some water, here; what, ho!

Enter one with water.

Where's my spaniel Troilus? Sirrah, get you hence
And bid my cousin Ferdinand come hither:
                                        [*Exit Servant.*]
One, Kate, that you must kiss and be acquainted 145
     with.
Where are my slippers? Shall I have some water?
Come, Kate, and wash, and welcome heartily.—
You whoreson villain! will you let it fall?
                                        [*Strikes him.*]
     Kat. Patience, I pray you; 'twas a fault unwill- 150
     ing.
     Pet. A whoreson, beetleheaded, flap-eared knave!
Come, Kate, sit down; I know you have a stomach.
Will you give thanks, sweet Kate, or else shall I?—
What's this? mutton?   155
     1. Ser.   Ay.
     Pet.   Who brought it?
     Peter.   I.

163. **trenchers:** wooden platters.

164. **joltheads:** dunces; blockheads.

165. **be with you:** i.e., settle you; give you your punishment; **straight:** at once.

170. **choler:** the humor governing bad temper.

S.D. after l. 176. **severally:** from several directions.

182. **rates:** scolds.

Pet. 'Tis burnt; and so is all the meat.
What dogs are these! Where is the rascal cook?   160
How durst you, villains, bring it from the dresser,
And serve it thus to me that love it not?
                    [*Throws the meat about the stage.*]
There, take it to you, trenchers, cups, and all.
You heedless joltheads and unmannered slaves!
What, do you grumble? I'll be with you straight.   165
Kat. I pray you, husband, be not so disquiet:
The meat was well, if you were so contented.
Pet. I tell thee, Kate, 'twas burnt and dried away,
And I expressly am forbid to touch it,
For it engenders choler, planteth anger,   170
And better 'twere that both of us did fast,
Since, of ourselves, ourselves are choleric,
Than feed it with such overroasted flesh.
Be patient; tomorrow't shall be mended,
And for this night we'll fast for company.   175
Come, I will bring thee to thy bridal chamber.
                              Exeunt.

Enter Servants severally.

Nat. Peter, didst ever see the like?
Peter. He kills her in her own humor.

Enter Curtis, a Servant.

Gru. Where is he?
Cur. In her chamber, making a sermon of con-   180
tinency to her;
And rails and swears and rates, that she, poor soul,

186. **politicly:** shrewdly.

188. **sharp:** eager (for food).

189. **stoop:** (1) swoop (from a height to snatch her prey), (2) submit.

190. **lure:** bait used by the falconer to entice the falcon back to his hand.

191. **man:** tame; **haggard:** undisciplined female hawk.

193. **watch:** deprive of sleep.

194. **bate:** flap their wings in agitation.

201. **intend:** pretend.

202. **reverend:** respectful.

208. **shrew:** pronounced "shrow" and sometimes so spelled.

Knows not which way to stand, to look, to speak,
And sits as one new-risen from a dream.
Away, away! for he is coming hither.   [*Exeunt.*] 185

Enter Petruchio.

Pet. Thus have I politicly begun my reign,
And 'tis my hope to end successfully.
My falcon now is sharp and passing empty,
And till she stoop she must not be full gorged,
For then she never looks upon her lure.   190
Another way I have to man my haggard,
To make her come and know her keeper's call;
That is, to watch her as we watch these kites
That bate and beat and will not be obedient.
She eat no meat today, nor none shall eat;   195
Last night she slept not, nor tonight she shall not:
As with the meat, some undeserved fault
I'll find about the making of the bed,
And here I'll fling the pillow, there the bolster,
This way the coverlet, another way the sheets.   200
Ay, and amid this hurly I intend
That all is done in reverend care of her,
And in conclusion she shall watch all night;
And if she chance to nod I'll rail and brawl
And with the clamor keep her still awake.   205
This is a way to kill a wife with kindness,
And thus I'll curb her mad and headstrong humor.
He that knows better how to tame a shrew,
Now let him speak: 'tis charity to show.

                                        Exit.

[IV. ii.] Hortensio and Tranio observe evidence of Bianca's partiality for Lucentio, and Tranio encourages Hortensio to forswear his suit by promising to do likewise. Hortensio resolves to marry a wealthy widow who loves him. The field is now open for Lucentio. Biondello has been assigned to find an elderly man to impersonate Lucentio's father in order that the marriage portion may be confirmed to Baptista's satisfaction. A traveling scholar who happens along is duped into undertaking the role of the wealthy Vincentio of Pisa; Tranio and Biondello hurry him off to Baptista's house.

‖‖‖‖‖‖‖‖‖‖‖‖‖‖‖‖‖‖‖‖‖‖‖‖‖

4. **bears me fair in hand:** pretends to encourage me.

9. **resolve:** inform; satisfy.

11. **the Art to Love:** i.e., Ovid's work on the subject.

15. **marry:** to be sure.

[Scene II. Padua. Before Baptista's house.]

Enter Tranio [(*Lucentio*)] *and Hortensio* [(*Licio*)].

    Tra./Luc. Is't possible, friend Licio, that Mistress
Bianca
Doth fancy any other but Lucentio?
I tell you, sir, she bears me fair in hand.
    Hor./Lic. Sir, to satisfy you in what I have said,   5
Stand by and mark the manner of his teaching.

    Enter Bianca [*and Lucentio* (*Cambio*)].

    Luc./Cam. Now, mistress, profit you in what you
read?
    Bia. What, master, read you? First resolve me
that.   10
    Luc./Cam. I read that I profess, the Art to Love.
    Bia. And may you prove, sir, master of your art!
    Luc./Cam. While you, sweet dear, prove mistress
of my heart.
    Hor./Lic. Quick proceeders, marry! Now, tell me,   15
I pray,
You that durst swear that your mistress Bianca
Loved none in the world so well as Lucentio.
    Tra./Luc. O despiteful love! unconstant woman-
kind!   20
I tell thee, Licio, this is wonderful.
    Hor./Lic. Mistake no more: I am not Licio,

26. **cullion:** base wretch.
30. **lightness:** inconstancy.
38. **fondly:** foolishly.
47. **haggard:** creature hard to tame; see [IV.i.] 191.

Nor a musician, as I seem to be;
But one that scorns to live in this disguise
For such a one as leaves a gentleman   25
And makes a god of such a cullion.
Know, sir, that I am called Hortensio.

   Tra./Luc. Signior Hortensio, I have often heard
Of your entire affection to Bianca,
And since mine eyes are witness of her lightness,   30
I will with you, if you be so contented,
Forswear Bianca and her love forever.

   Hor./Lic. See how they kiss and court! Signior
    Lucentio,
Here is my hand and here I firmly vow   35
Never to woo her more, but do forswear her,
As one unworthy all the former favors
That I have fondly flattered her withal.

   Tra./Luc. And here I take the like unfeigned oath,
Never to marry with her though she would entreat.   40
Fie on her! see how beastly she doth court him.

   Hor./Lic. Would all the world but he had quite
    forsworn!
For me, that I may surely keep mine oath,
I will be married to a wealthy widow   45
Ere three days pass, which hath as long loved me
As I have loved this proud disdainful haggard.
And so farewell, Signior Lucentio.
Kindness in women, not their beauteous looks,
Shall win my love; and so I take my leave   50
In resolution as I swore before.   [*Exit.*]

54. **longeth:** belongeth.

70. **tricks eleven-and-twenty long:** thirty-one tricks (alluding to the card game "Trentuno"); tricks adequate to win.

74. **ancient angel:** like the old coin (**angel**), sound and trustworthy.

77. **mercatante:** old Italian for "merchant"; **pedant:** scholar. Both wealthy merchants and scholars wore similar dark gowns.

Tra./Luc. Mistress Bianca, bless you with such
    grace
As longeth to a lover's blessed case!
Nay, I have ta'en you napping, gentle love,   55
And have forsworn you with Hortensio.

Bia. Tranio, you jest. But have you both forsworn
    me?

Tra./Luc. Mistress, we have.

Luc./Cam.   Then we are rid of Licio.   60

Tra./Luc. I' faith, he'll have a lusty widow now,
That shall be wooed and wedded in a day.

Bia. God give him joy!

Tra./Luc. Ay, and he'll tame her.

Bia.   He says so, Tranio.   65

Tra./Luc. Faith, he is gone unto the taming school.

Bia. The taming school! What, is there such a
    place?

Tra./Luc. Ay, mistress, and Petruchio is the master,
That teacheth tricks eleven-and-twenty long   70
To tame a shrew and charm her chattering tongue.

Enter Biondello.

Bio. O master, master! I have watched so long
That I'm dog-weary, but at last I spied
An ancient angel coming down the hill
Will serve the turn.   75

Tra./Luc.   What is he, Biondello?

Bio. Master, a *mercatante* or a pedant—
I know not what; but formal in apparel,
In gait and countenance surely like a father.

85. **let me alone:** i.e., leave the matter to me.

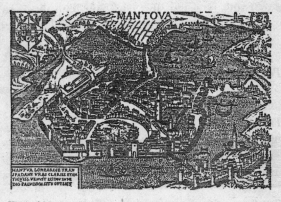

View of Mantua. From Pietro Bertelli, *Theatrum urbium Italicarum*
(1599).

Luc./Cam. And what of him, Tranio?   80
   Tra./Luc. If he be credulous and trust my tale
I'll make him glad to seem Vincentio,
And give assurance to Baptista Minola
As if he were the right Vincentio.
Take in your love and then let me alone.   85
      [*Exeunt Lucentio (Cambio) and Bianca.*]

Enter a Pedant.

  Ped. God save you, sir!
   Tra./Luc.   And you, sir! You are welcome.
Travel you far on, or are you at the farthest?
  Ped. Sir, at the farthest for a week or two,
But then up farther and as far as Rome;   90
And so to Tripoli, if God lend me life.
   Tra./Luc. What countryman, I pray?
  Ped.   Of Mantua.
   Tra./Luc. Of Mantua, sir! Marry, God forbid!
And come to Padua, careless of your life?   95
  Ped. My life, sir! How, I pray? for that goes hard.
   Tra./Luc. 'Tis death for anyone in Mantua
To come to Padua. Know you not the cause?
Your ships are stayed at Venice, and the Duke—
For private quarrel 'twixt your duke and him—   100
Hath published and proclaimed it openly.
'Tis marvel, but that you are but newly come,
You might have heard it else proclaimed about.
  Ped. Alas, sir! it is worse for me than so,
For I have bills for money by exchange   105
From Florence and must here deliver them.

115. **sooth:** truth.
118. **all one:** i.e., it makes no difference.
123. **undertake:** assume.
125. **take upon you:** conduct yourself.
135. **pass assurance of:** confirm.

Tra./Luc. Well, sir, to do you courtesy,
This will I do and this I will advise you:
First, tell me, have you ever been at Pisa?

Ped. Ay, sir, in Pisa have I often been;   110
Pisa, renowned for grave citizens.

Tra./Luc. Among them, know you one Vincentio?

Ped. I know him not but I have heard of him;
A merchant of incomparable wealth.

Tra./Luc. He is my father, sir; and, sooth to say,   115
In count'nance somewhat doth resemble you.

Bio. [*Aside*] As much as an apple doth an oyster,
and all one.

Tra./Luc. To save your life in this extremity,
This favor will I do you for his sake,   120
And think it not the worst of all your fortunes
That you are like to Sir Vincentio.
His name and credit shall you undertake,
And in my house you shall be friendly lodged.
Look that you take upon you as you should!   125
You understand me, sir; so shall you stay
Till you have done your business in the city.
If this be court'sy, sir, accept of it.

Ped. O sir, I do; and will repute you ever
The patron of my life and liberty.   130

Tra./Luc. Then go with me to make the matter
      good.
This, by the way, I let you understand:
My father is here looked for every day
To pass assurance of a dower in marriage   135
'Twixt me and one Baptista's daughter here.

[**IV. iii.**] Petruchio's taming process is beginning to break Katherina, who has been kept sleepless and hungry by his unreasonable concern for her welfare. Although he promises her that they will now go to visit her father dressed in proper finery, he finds fault with the cap and gown the tailor has made according to instructions, and refuses to accept them. They will go in the poor clothing they have on, he announces; after all, it is the mind that makes the body rich.

6. **present:** immediate.
14. **As who should say:** as if to say.
18. **neat's:** calf's.

In all these circumstances I'll instruct you.
Go with me to clothe you as becomes you.

Exeunt.

Scene [III. A room in Petruchio's house.]

Enter Katherina and Grumio.

Gru. No, no, forsooth; I dare not for my life.
Kat. The more my wrong, the more his spite ap-
     pears.
What, did he marry me to famish me?
Beggars, that come unto my father's door,   5
Upon entreaty have a present alms;
If not, elsewhere they meet with charity.
But I, who never knew how to entreat,
Nor never needed that I should entreat,
Am starved for meat, giddy for lack of sleep,   10
With oaths kept waking and with brawling fed.
And that which spites me more than all these wants,
He does it under name of perfect love,
As who should say, if I should sleep or eat
'Twere deadly sickness or else present death.   15
I prithee go and get me some repast;
I care not what, so it be wholesome food.
     Gru. What say you to a neat's foot?
     Kat. 'Tis passing good; I prithee let me have it.
     Gru. I fear it is too choleric a meat.   20
How say you to a fat tripe finely broiled?

34. **very:** mere.
38–9. **all amort:** French *à la mort;* dispirited.
44. **dress:** prepare.
47. **sorted to no proof:** attended by no result.

Kat. I like it well; good Grumio, fetch it me.

Gru. I cannot tell; I fear 'tis choleric.

What say you to a piece of beef and mustard?

    Kat. A dish that I do love to feed upon.   25

    Gru. Ay, but the mustard is too hot a little.

    Kat. Why then, the beef, and let the mustard rest.

    Gru. Nay then, I will not; you shall have the mustard

Or else you get no beef of Grumio.   30

    Kat. Then both, or one, or anything thou wilt.

    Gru. Why then, the mustard without the beef.

    Kat. Go, get thee gone, thou false deluding slave,

                          Beats him.

That feedst me with the very name of meat.

Sorrow on thee and all the pack of you   35

That triumph thus upon my misery!

Go, get thee gone, I say.

    Enter Petruchio, and Hortensio with meat.

    Pet. How fares my Kate? What, sweeting, all amort?

    Hor. Mistress, what cheer?   40

    Kat. -   Faith, as cold as can be.

    Pet. Pluck up thy spirits; look cheerfully upon me.

Here, love; thou seest how diligent I am

To dress thy meat myself and bring it thee.

I am sure, sweet Kate, this kindness merits thanks.   45

What! not a word? Nay then, thou lovest it not

And all my pains is sorted to no proof.

Here, take away this dish.

61. **farthingales:** hooped petticoats.

64. **stays:** awaits.

65. **ruffling:** swaggering.

69. **bespeak:** order.

71. **lewd:** base; **filthy:** disgusting.

73. **knack:** knickknack; **toy:** synonymous with **trick:** trifle.

MATRONA PADOVANA.

"Ruffs and cuffs and farthingales and things." From Cesare Vecellio, *De gli habiti antichi et moderni* (1590).

Kat.   I pray you, let it stand.

Pet. The poorest service is repaid with thanks,   50
And so shall mine, before you touch the meat.

Kat. I thank you, sir.

Hor. Signior Petruchio, fie! you are to blame.
Come, Mistress Kate, I'll bear you company.

Pet. Eat it up all, Hortensio, if thou lovest me.   55
Much good do it unto thy gentle heart!
Kate, eat apace. And now, my honey love,
Will we return unto thy father's house
And revel it as bravely as the best,
With silken coats and caps and golden rings,   60
With ruffs and cuffs and farthingales and things;
With scarfs and fans and double change of brav'ry,
With amber bracelets, beads, and all this knav'ry.
What! hast thou dined? The tailor stays thy leisure
To deck thy body with his ruffling treasure.   65

Enter Tailor.

Come, tailor, let us see these ornaments;
Lay forth the gown.

Enter Haberdasher.

                 What news with you, sir?

Hab. Here is the cap your Worship did bespeak.

Pet. Why, this was molded on a porringer;   70
A velvet dish: fie, fie! 'tis lewd and filthy:
Why, 'tis a cockle or a walnut shell,
A knack, a toy, a trick, a baby's cap—
Away with it! Come, let me have a bigger.

75. **fit the time:** conform to fashion.

86. **free:** outspoken.

89. **custard-coffin:** pasty shell.

94. **masquing stuff:** masquerade finery.

95. **demicannon:** a cannon with a bore of about 6½ inches. The **demicannon** sleeve, popular in the late sixteenth century, was shaped like a cannon in being tapered from the shoulder to the cuff; inner stiffening was used to maintain a full shape.

98. **censer:** brazier with perforated top, in which perfume was burned.

100. **like:** likely.

Kat. I'll have no bigger, this doth fit the time,   75
And gentlewomen wear such caps as these.

Pet. When you are gentle you shall have one too—
And not till then.

Hor. [*Aside*] That will not be in haste.

Kat. Why, sir, I trust I may have leave to speak,   80
And speak I will; I am no child, no babe.
Your betters have endured me say my mind,
And if you cannot, best you stop your ears.
My tongue will tell the anger of my heart,
Or else my heart, concealing it, will break,   85
And rather than it shall, I will be free,
Even to the uttermost, as I please, in words.

Pet. Why, thou sayst true; it is a paltry cap,
A custard-coffin, a bauble, a silken pie.
I love thee well in that thou likest it not.   90

Kat. Love me or love me not, I like the cap,
And it I will have or I will have none.

[*Exit Haberdasher.*]

Pet. Thy gown? Why, ay: come, tailor, let us see't.
O mercy, God! what masquing stuff is here?
What's this? a sleeve? 'Tis like a demicannon.   95
What! up and down, carved like an apple tart?
Here's snip and nip and cut and slish and slash,
Like to a censer in a barber's shop.
Why, what, a devil's name, tailor, callst thou this?

Hor. [*Aside*] I see, she's like to have neither cap   100
    nor gown.

Tai. You bid me make it orderly and well,
According to the fashion and the time.

104. **Marry, and did:** so I did; **be rememb'red:** recall.

106. **kennel:** gutter.

110. **quaint:** elegant.

117. **nail:** a cloth measure of 2¼ inches.

119. **Braved:** defied; **with:** by.

121. **bemete:** be-measure; i.e., beat.

122. **think on prating whilst thou livest:** i.e., never forget your boastful talk.

131. **faced:** (1) trimmed, (2) brazened out.

133. **Face:** oppose hostilely; **braved:** made brave (fine).

Pet. Marry, and did; but if you be rememb'red,
I did not bid you mar it to the time.   105
Go, hop me over every kennel home,
For you shall hop without my custom, sir.
I'll none of it: hence! make your best of it.
  Kat. I never saw a better-fashioned gown,
More quaint, more pleasing, nor more commendable. 110
Belike you mean to make a puppet of me.
  Pet. Why, true; he means to make a puppet of thee.
  Tai. She says your Worship means to make a pup-
    pet of her.
  Pet. O monstrous arrogance!   115
Thou liest, thou thread, thou thimble,
Thou yard, three-quarters, half yard, quarter, nail!
Thou flea, thou nit, thou winter cricket thou!
Braved in mine own house with a skein of thread!
Away! thou rag, thou quantity, thou remnant,   120
Or I shall so bemete thee with thy yard
As thou shalt think on prating whilst thou livest!
I tell thee, I, that thou hast marred her gown.
  Tai. Your Worship is deceived; the gown is made
Just as my master had direction.   125
Grumio gave order how it should be done.
  Gru. I gave him no order; I gave him the stuff.
  Tai. But how did you desire it should be made?
  Gru. Marry, sir, with needle and thread.
  Tai. But did you not request to have it cut?   130
  Gru. Thou hast faced many things.
  Tai. I have.
  Gru. Face not me: thou hast braved many men;

134. **brave:** defy (as at line 119).

136. **ergo:** therefore; a favorite "learned" word with Elizabethan clowns.

141. **loose-bodied gown:** a common article of feminine clothing, usually for wear at home, but also an innuendo for a loose woman.

143. **bottom:** i.e., the spool on which the thread was wound.

145. **compassed:** circular.

147. **trunk sleeve:** a full sleeve; the **demicannon** was of this type.

149. **curiously:** ingeniously.

157. **bill:** with a pun on the weapon of that name.

158. **meteyard:** yardstick.

DONNE PRINCIPA-
LI

A loose-bodied gown. From Cesare Vecellio, *De gli habiti antichi et moderni* (1590).

brave not me: I will neither be faced nor braved. I
say unto thee, I bid thy master cut out the gown, but   135
I did not bid him cut it to pieces; *ergo*, thou liest.

Tai. Why, here is the note of the fashion to testify.

Pet. Read it.

Gru. The note lies in's throat if he say I said so.

Tai. "*Imprimis*, a loose-bodied gown."   140

Gru. Master, if ever I said loose-bodied gown, sew
me in the skirts of it and beat me to death with a
bottom of brown thread. I said a gown.

Pet. Proceed.

Tai. "With a small compassed cape."   145

Gru. I confess the cape.

Tai. "With a trunk sleeve."

Gru. I confess two sleeves.

Tai. "The sleeves curiously cut."

Pet. Ay, there's the villainy.   150

Gru. Error i' the bill, sir; error i' the bill! I commanded the sleeves should be cut out and sewed up
again, and that I'll prove upon thee, though thy little
finger be armed in a thimble.

Tai. This is true that I say; and I had thee in place   155
where, thou shouldst know it.

Gru. I am for thee straight. Take thou the bill, give
me thy meteyard, and spare not me.

Hor. God-a-mercy, Grumio! Then he shall have no
odds.   160

Pet. Well, sir, in brief, the gown is not for me.

Gru. You are i' the right, sir; 'tis for my mistress.

Pet. Go, take it up unto thy master's use.

166. **conceit:** idea; fancy.

175. **commend me:** offer my greetings.

182. **peereth:** shows through; **habit:** attire.

188. **furniture:** outfittings; clothing and accessories.

Gru. Villain, not for thy life! Take up my mistress'
gown for thy master's use!   165

Pet. Why, sir, what's your conceit in that?

Gru. O, sir, the conceit is deeper than you think for.
Take up my mistress' gown to his master's use!
O, fie, fie, fie!

Pet. [*Aside*] Hortensio, say thou wilt see the tailor 170
    paid.
Go take it hence; be gone and say no more.

Hor. Tailor, I'll pay thee for thy gown tomorrow;
Take no unkindness of his hasty words.
Away! I say; commend me to thy master. *Exit Tailor.* 175

Pet. Well, come, my Kate; we will unto your
    father's,
Even in these honest mean habiliments.
Our purses shall be proud, our garments poor,
For 'tis the mind that makes the body rich;   180
And as the sun breaks through the darkest clouds,
So honor peereth in the meanest habit.
What, is the jay more precious than the lark
Because his feathers are more beautiful?
Or is the adder better than the eel   185
Because his painted skin contents the eye?
O, no, good Kate; neither art thou the worse
For this poor furniture and mean array.
If thou accountst it shame, lay it on me.
And therefore frolic; we will hence forthwith   190
To feast and sport us at thy father's house.
Go call my men, and let us straight to him;

200. **Look what:** whatever.
201. **still:** ever.

⁃⁃⁃⁃⁃⁃⁃⁃⁃⁃⁃⁃⁃⁃⁃⁃⁃⁃⁃⁃⁃⁃⁃⁃⁃⁃⁃⁃⁃⁃⁃⁃⁃⁃⁃⁃

[**IV. iv.**] Tranio, with the pedant disguised as Vincentio, calls upon Baptista, who agrees to draw up terms of marriage between Lucentio (in the person of Tranio) and Bianca. Biondello secretly counsels the real Lucentio to lose no time in marrying Bianca himself.

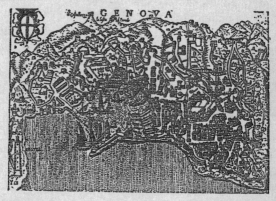

View of Genoa. From Pietro Bertelli, *Theatrum urbium Italicarum* (1599).

And bring our horses unto Long-Lane end;
There will we mount, and thither walk on foot.
Let's see; I think 'tis now some seven o'clock,   195
And well we may come there by dinnertime.

    Kat. I dare assure you, sir, 'tis almost two
And 'twill be suppertime ere you come there.

    Pet. It shall be seven ere I go to horse.
Look what I speak or do or think to do,   200
You are still crossing it. Sirs, let't alone:
I will not go today; and ere I do,
It shall be what o'clock I say it is.

    Hor. Why, so this gallant will command the sun.
                                 Exeunt.

[Scene IV. Padua. Before Baptista's house.]

*Enter Tranio [(Lucentio)], and the Pedant dressed
    like Vincentio (booted and bareheaded).*

    Tra./Luc. Sir, this is the house: please it you that I
    call?

    Ped. Ay, what else? And, but I be deceived,
Signior Baptista may remember me,
Near twenty years ago, in Genoa,   5
Where we were lodgers at the Pegasus.

    Tra./Luc. 'Tis well; and hold your own in any case
With such austerity as longeth to a father.

    Ped. I warrant you.

13. **throughly:** thoroughly.
14. **right:** genuine.
20. **tall:** splendid; fine.
23. **happily:** fortunately.

Enter Biondello.

                  But, sir, here comes your boy;   10
'Twere good he were schooled.
   Tra./Luc. Fear you not him. Sirrah Biondello,
Now do your duty throughly, I advise you:
Imagine 'twere the right Vincentio.
   Bio. Tut! fear not me.   15
   Tra./Luc. But hast thou done thy errand to
     Baptista?
   Bio. I told him that your father was at Venice,
And that you looked for him this day in Padua.
   Tra./Luc. Th' art a tall fellow: hold thee that to   20
     drink.   *[Gives him a coin.]*
Here comes Baptista. Set your countenance, sir.

Enter Baptista and Lucentio [(Cambio)].

Signior Baptista, you are happily met.
[To the Pedant] Sir, this is the gentleman I told you
   of.   25
I pray you, stand good father to me now,
Give me Bianca for my patrimony.
   Ped. Soft, son!
Sir, by your leave: having come to Padua
To gather in some debts, my son Lucentio   30
Made me acquainted with a weighty cause
Of love between your daughter and himself.

36. **in a good father's care:** as befits the care of a good father.

41. **curious:** minutely particular.

50. **pass:** guarantee.

55. **affied:** formally betrothed.

60. **happily;** haply; perhaps.

61. **like:** please.

And—for the good report I hear of you,
And for the love he beareth to your daughter,
And she to him—to stay him not too long,   35
I am content, in a good father's care,
To have him matched; and if you please to like
No worse than I, upon some agreement
Me shall you find ready and willing
With one consent to have her so bestowed;   40
For curious I cannot be with you,
Signior Baptista, of whom I hear so well.

   Bap. Sir, pardon me in what I have to say:
Your plainness and your shortness please me well.
Right true it is, your son Lucentio here   45
Doth love my daughter and she loveth him—
Or both dissemble deeply their affections—
And therefore, if you say no more than this,
That like a father you will deal with him
And pass my daughter a sufficient dower,   50
The match is made; and all is done;
Your son shall have my daughter with consent.

   Tra./Luc. I thank you, sir. Where, then, do you
     know best
We be affied and such assurance ta'en   55
As shall with either part's agreement stand?

   Bap. Not in my house, Lucentio; for, you know,
Pitchers have ears, and I have many servants.
Besides, old Gremio is heark'ning still,
And happily we might be interrupted.   60

   Tra./Luc. Then at my lodging, and it like you:
There doth my father lie, and there this night

65. **scrivener:** clerk; notary.

67. **pittance:** i.e., allowance of victuals.

78. **mess:** course; **cheer:** fare (at the bridal meal).

86. **has:** he has.

89. **moralize:** explain.

We'll pass the business privately and well.
Send for your daughter by your servant here;
My boy shall fetch the scrivener presently.   65
The worst is this, that, at so slender warning,
You are like to have a thin and slender pittance.

   Bap. It likes me well. Cambio, hie you home
And bid Bianca make her ready straight;
And, if you will, tell what hath happened: 70
Lucentio's father is arrived in Padua,
And how she's like to be Lucentio's wife.

   Luc./Cam. I pray the gods she may with all my
      heart!   *Exit* [*Lucentio*].
   Tra./Luc. Dally not with the gods, but get thee   75
      gone.   [*Exit Biondello*.]
Signior Baptista, shall I lead the way?
Welcome! one mess is like to be your cheer.
Come, sir; we will better it in Pisa.

   Bap. I follow you.   *Exeunt.*   80

   Enter Lucentio (Cambio) and Biondello.

   Bio. Cambio!
   Luc./Cam. What sayst thou, Biondello?
   Bio. You saw my master wink and laugh upon
you?
   Luc./Cam. Biondello, what of that?   85
   Bio. Faith, nothing; but has left me here behind
to expound the meaning or moral of his signs and
tokens.
   Luc./Cam. I pray thee, moralize them.

100. **assurance:** marriage engagement.

101. **cum privilegio ad imprimendum solum:** with the privilege of exclusive printing; a phrase used in conferring the right to print.

112. **against:** before.

113. **appendix:** appendage (his wife-to-be).

116. **roundly:** straightforwardly.

117. **It shall go hard:** i.e., the difficulties will have to be insuperable.

Bio. Then thus. Baptista is safe, talking with the   90
deceiving father of a deceitful son.

Luc./Cam. And what of him?

Bio. His daughter is to be brought by you to the
supper.

Luc./Cam. And then?   95

Bio. The old priest at Saint Luke's Church is at
your command at all hours.

Luc./Cam. And what of all this?

Bio. I cannot tell, except they are busied about
a counterfeit assurance: take you assurance of her,   100
cum privilegio ad imprimendum solum. To the
church! Take the priest, clerk, and some sufficient
honest witnesses.
If this be not that you look for, I have no more to
   say,   105
But bid Bianca farewell forever and a day.

Luc./Cam. Hearest thou, Biondello?

Bio. I cannot tarry: I knew a wench married in
an afternoon as she went to the garden for parsley
to stuff a rabbit; and so may you, sir; and so, adieu,   110
sir. My master hath appointed me to go to Saint
Luke's, to bid the priest be ready to come against you
come with your appendix.   *Exit.*

Luc./Cam. I may, and will, if she be so contented.
She will be pleased; then wherefore should I doubt?   115
Hap what hap may, I'll roundly go about her;
It shall go hard if Cambio go without her.

                                        Exit.

[IV. v.] En route to Baptista's house, Petruchio completes his conquest of Katherina's spirit by bullying her into agreeing that the sun is the moon and the elderly Vincentio, whom they meet on the road, is a fair young girl. When Vincentio identifies himself as the father of Lucentio, Petruchio informs him that they are probably related by marriage, since by this time Lucentio should have married Bianca. The spectacle of Katherina's submission has encouraged Hortensio in the belief that he can control his widow.

‖‖‖‖‖‖‖‖‖‖‖‖‖‖‖‖‖‖‖‖‖‖

1. **a:** in.
11. **Or ere:** before.
18. **rush candle:** a candle made of a rush dipped in grease.

[Scene V. A public road.]

Enter Petruchio, Kate, Hortensio, [and Servants].

   Pet. Come on, a God's name; once more toward
     our father's.
Good Lord, how bright and goodly shines the
     moon!
   Kat. The moon! The sun: it is not moonlight now.   5
   Pet. I say it is the moon that shines so bright.
   Kat. I know it is the sun that shines so bright.
   Pet. Now, by my mother's son, and that's my-
     self,
It shall be moon, or star, or what I list,   10
Or ere I journey to your father's house.
Go on and fetch our horses back again.
Evermore crossed and crossed; nothing but crossed!
   Hor. Say as he says, or we shall never go.
   Kat. Forward, I pray, since we have come so   15
     far,
And be it moon, or sun, or what you please.
And if you please to call it a rush candle,
Henceforth I vow it shall be so for me.
   Pet. I say it is the moon.   20
   Kat.   I know it is the moon.
   Pet. Nay, then you lie; it is the blessed sun.
   Kat. Then God be blest, it is the blessed sun!
But sun it is not when you say it is not,
And the moon changes even as your mind.   25

29. **bowl:** bowling ball.

31. **against the bias:** crosswise; contrarily. The bias of a bowl was the lead weight in the construction of one side to cause it to swerve around an opponent's ball when correctly bowled.

36. **fresher:** more blooming.

42. **'A:** he.

What you will have it named, even that it is;
And so it shall be so for Katherine.
  Hor. Petruchio, go thy ways; the field is won.
  Pet. Well, forward, forward! Thus the bowl should
    run   30
And not unluckily against the bias.
But soft! company is coming here.

Enter Vincentio.

[*To Vincentio*] Good morrow, gentle mistress: where
    away?
Tell me, sweet Kate, and tell me truly too,   35
Hast thou beheld a fresher gentlewoman?
Such war of white and red within her cheeks!
What stars do spangle heaven with such beauty
As those two eyes become that heavenly face?
Fair lovely maid, once more good day to thee.   40
Sweet Kate, embrace her for her beauty's sake.
  Hor. 'A will make the man mad, to make a woman
    of him.
  Kat. Young budding virgin, fair and fresh and
    sweet,   45
Whither away, or where is thy abode?
Happy the parents of so fair a child;
Happier the man, whom favorable stars
Allot thee for his lovely bedfellow!
  Pet. Why, how now, Kate! I hope thou art not   50
    mad;
This is a man, old, wrinkled, faded, withered,
And not a maiden, as thou sayst he is.

57. **reverend:** venerable.

64. **encounter:** greeting.

74. **this:** this time.

77. **qualified:** endowed with qualities; **beseem:** befit.

83. **pleasant:** facetious.

Kat. Pardon, old father, my mistaking eyes,
That have been so bedazzled with the sun   55
That everything I look on seemeth green.
Now I perceive thou art a reverend father;
Pardon, I pray thee, for my mad mistaking.

Pet. Do, good old grandsire; and withal make
    known   60
Which way thou travelest: if along with us,
We shall be joyful of thy company.

Vin. Fair sir, and you my merry mistress,
That with your strange encounter much amazed me,
My name is called Vincentio; my dwelling, Pisa;   65
And bound I am to Padua, there to visit
A son of mine, which long I have not seen.

Pet. What is his name?

Vin.   Lucentio, gentle sir.

Pet. Happily met; the happier for thy son.   70
And now by law, as well as reverend age,
I may entitle thee my loving father:
The sister to my wife, this gentlewoman,
Thy son by this hath married. Wonder not
Nor be not grieved: she is of good esteem,   75
Her dowry wealthy, and of worthy birth;
Beside, so qualified as may beseem
The spouse of any noble gentleman.
Let me embrace with old Vincentio
And wander we to see thy honest son,   80
Who will of thy arrival be full joyous.

Vin. But is this true? or is it else your pleasure,
Like pleasant travelers, to break a jest

87. **jealous:** suspicious.

89. **Have to my widow:** let my window beware.

90. **untoward:** synonymous with **froward;** intractable.

Upon the company you overtake?

  Hor. I do assure thee, father, so it is.   85

  Pet. Come, go along, and see the truth hereof;

For our first merriment hath made thee jealous.

                  Exeunt [all but Hortensio].

  Hor. Well, Petruchio, this has put me in heart.

Have to my widow! and if she be froward,

Then hast thou taught Hortensio to be untoward.   90

                        Exit.

THE
TAMING OF
THE SHREW

ACT V

[V. i.] While Lucentio and Bianca are being secretly married, Petruchio and his company arrive at Lucentio's house and find the pseudo-Vincentio already there. Biondello and Tranio try to bluff out the situation, but the real Vincentio is acknowledged when Lucentio himself enters with his bride, asks his father's pardon, and explains the masquerade.

<hr />

Ent. **Gremio is out before:** Gremio is at the front of the stage when the others enter behind him, so that he is unaware of their presence.

5. **a:** on. Biondello means that he will see Lucentio safely into the church.

10. **bears:** stands.

15. **toward:** likely to be offered.

[ACT V]

[Scene I. Padua. Before Lucentio's house.]

Enter Biondello, Lucentio, and Bianca;
Gremio is out before.

Bio. Softly and swiftly, sir, for the priest is
ready.

Luc. I fly, Biondello, but they may chance to need
thee at home; therefore leave us.

Exit [with Bianca].

Bio. Nay, faith, I'll see the church a your back;   5
and then come back to my master's as soon as I
can.   *[Exit.]*

Gre. I marvel Cambio comes not all this while.

Enter Petruchio, Kate, Vincentio, [and] Grumio
with Attendants.

Pet. Sir, here's the door, this is Lucentio's house:
My father's bears more toward the market place;   10
Thither must I, and here I leave you, sir.

Vin. You shall not choose but drink before you
go.
I think I shall command your welcome here,
And, by all likelihood, some cheer is toward. *Knock.* 15

93

28–9. **To leave frivolous circumstances:** having done with trivial details.

38. **flat:** plain; downright.

41–2. **cozen:** cheat; **under my countenance:** in my semblance.

Gre. They're busy within; you were best knock
louder.

Pedant looks out of the window.

Ped. What's he that knocks as he would beat down
the gate?

Vin. Is Signior Lucentio within, sir?　20

Ped. He's within, sir, but not to be spoken withal.

Vin. What if a man bring him a hundred pound
or two, to make merry withal?

Ped. Keep your hundred pounds to yourself; he　25
shall need none so long as I live.

Pet. Nay, I told you your son was well beloved in Padua. Do you hear, sir? To leave frivolous
circumstances, I pray you tell Signior Lucentio that
his father is come from Pisa and is here at the door　30
to speak with him.

Ped. Thou liest; his father is come from Padua and
here looking out at the window.

Vin. Art thou his father?

Ped. Ay, sir, so his mother says, if I may believe　35
her.

Pet. [*To Vincentio*] Why, how now, gentleman!
Why, this is flat knavery, to take upon you another
man's name.

Ped. Lay hands on the villain; I believe 'a means　40
to cozen somebody in this city under my countenance.

47. **crackhemp:** gallows bird.
55. **worshipful:** distinguished.

Enter Biondello.

Bio. I have seen them in the church together;
God send 'em good shipping! But who is here? Mine
old master, Vincentio! Now we are undone and   45
brought to nothing.

Vin. Come hither, crackhemp.

Bio. I hope I may choose, sir.

Vin. Come hither, you rogue. What, have you
forgot me?   50

Bio. Forgot you! No, sir. I could not forget you,
for I never saw you before in all my life.

Vin. What, you notorious villain! Didst thou never
see thy master's father, Vincentio?

Bio. What, my old, worshipful old master? Yes,   55
marry, sir: see where he looks out of the window.

Vin. Is't so, indeed?   *He beats Biondello.*

Bio. Help, help, help! Here's a madman will mur-
der me.   *[Exit.]*

Ped. Help, son! Help, Signior Baptista!   60
               [Exit from above.]

Pet. Prithee, Kate, let's stand aside and see the
end of this controversy.   *[They retire.]*

*Enter Pedant [below] with Servants, Baptista,
    [and] Tranio [(Lucentio)].*

Tra./Luc. Sir, what are you that offer to beat my
servant?

66. **fine villain:** finely-dressed menial. **Villain** originally meant simply a baseborn person.

67. **hose:** pair of breeches; **copatain hat:** a high conical hat.

74. **habit:** apparel.

75. **cerns:** concerns.

76. **maintain:** afford.

78. **Bergamo:** actually not a port but a village in central Lombardy.

Men gaming. The two at left wear copatain hats. From J. J. Boissard, *Emblematum liber* (1593).

Vin. What am I, sir! Nay, what are you, sir?   65
O immortal gods! O fine villain! A silken doublet!
a velvet hose! a scarlet cloak! and a copatain hat!
O, I am undone! I am undone! While I play the good
husband at home, my son and my servant spend all
at the university.   70

Tra./Luc. How now! what's the matter?

Bap. What, is the man lunatic?

Tra./Luc. Sir, you seem a sober ancient gentleman
by your habit, but your words show you a madman.
Why, sir, what cerns it you if I wear pearl and gold?   75
I thank my good father, I am able to maintain it.

Vin. Thy father! O villain! He is a sailmaker in
Bergamo.

Bap. You mistake, sir, you mistake, sir. Pray, what
do you think is his name?   80

Vin. His name! As if I knew not his name! I have
brought him up ever since he was three years old,
and his name is Tranio.

Ped. Away, away, mad ass! his name is Lucentio
and he is mine only son, and heir to the lands of me,   85
Signior Vincentio.

Vin. Lucentio! O he hath murd'red his master.
Lay hold on him, I charge you in the Duke's name.
O my son, my son! Tell me, thou villain, where is my
son Lucentio?   90

Tra./Luc. Call forth an officer.

99. **cony-catched:** tricked.
108. **haled:** vexed.

View of Bergamo. From Pietro Bertelli, *Theatrum urbium Italicarum* (1599).

[Enter one with an Officer.]

Carry this mad knave to the jail. Father Baptista, I
charge you see that he be forthcoming.

Vin. Carry me to the jail!

Gre. Stay, officer: he shall not go to prison.   95

Bap. Talk not, Signior Gremio. I say he shall go
to prison.

Gre. Take heed, Signior Baptista, lest you be
cony-catched in this business. I dare swear this is the
right Vincentio.   100

Ped. Swear, if thou darest.

Gre. Nay, I dare not swear it.

Tra./Luc. Then thou wert best say that I am not
Lucentio.

Gre. Yes, I know thee to be Signior Lucentio.   105

Bap. Away with the dotard; to the jail with
him!

Vin. Thus strangers may be haled and abused;
O monstrous villain!

Enter Biondello, Lucentio, and Bianca.

Bio. O, we are spoiled; and yonder he is: deny 110
him, forswear him, or else we are all undone.

            Exeunt Biondello, Tranio, and Pedant as fast
                                      as may be.

Luc. Pardon, sweet father.   *Kneel.*

Vin.   Lives my sweet son?

120. **supposes:** imitations; **eyne:** eyes.

121. **packing:** plotting; **with a witness:** unmistakably.

138–39. **go to:** give over; don't be upset.

Bia. Pardon, dear father.

Bap.   How hast thou offended? 115
Where is Lucentio?

Luc.   Here's Lucentio,
Right son to the right Vincentio,
That have by marriage made thy daughter mine
While counterfeit supposes bleared thine eyne.   120

Gre. Here's packing, with a witness, to deceive us
all!

Vin. Where is that damned villain Tranio,
That faced and braved me in this matter so?

Bap. Why, tell me, is not this my Cambio?   125

Bia. Cambio is changed into Lucentio.

Luc. Love wrought these miracles. Bianca's love
Made me exchange my state with Tranio,
While he did bear my countenance in the town;
And happily I have arrived at the last   130
Unto the wished haven of my bliss.
What Tranio did, myself enforced him to;
Then pardon him, sweet father, for my sake.

Vin. I'll slit the villain's nose, that would have sent
me to the jail.   135

Bap. But do you hear, sir? Have you married my
daughter without asking my good will?

Vin. Fear not, Baptista; we will content you, go
to: but I will in, to be revenged for this villainy.

                                    Exit.

Bap. And I, to sound the depth of this knavery. 140
                                    Exit.

143. **My cake is dough:** I have failed; see [I. i.] 111–12.

144. **Out of hope of all:** hopeless of anything.

156. **Better once than never, for never too late:** "Better late than never."

⸻

[V. ii.] The three newly married couples, Petruchio and Katherina, Lucentio and Bianca, and Hortensio and his widow, are banqueting together. Petruchio has to endure some taunts about Katherina's shrewish disposition, but he wagers the other two husbands that of the three wives his own will be most obedient to his summons. His wager is won when both Bianca and the widow refuse to come at the bidding of Lucentio and Hortensio, while Katherina immediately obliges and at Petruchio's request escorts the other two women into their husband's presences. Katherina expresses her new philosophy that women owe it to their husbands and themselves to behave like the softer sex and repay their husbands' care and labor with proper wifely obedience. Petruchio is delighted and kisses her soundly. It is clear that the shrew promises to provide her husband with greater domestic bliss than the husbands of the sweet Bianca and the doting widow will enjoy.

⸻

3. **overblown:** past.

Luc. Look not pale, Bianca; thy father will not
frown.   *Exeunt* [*Lucentio and Bianca*].

Gre. My cake is dough, but I'll in among the rest,
Out of hope of all but my share of the feast.   [*Exit.*]

Kat. Husband, let's follow to see the end of this   145
    ado.

Pet. First kiss me, Kate, and we will.

Kat. What! in the midst of the street?

Pet. What! art thou ashamed of me?

Kat. No, sir, God forbid; but ashamed to kiss.   150

Pet. Why, then let's home again. Come, sirrah, let's
    away.

Kat. Nay, I will give thee a kiss; now pray thee,
    love, stay.

Pet. Is not this well? Come, my sweet Kate;   155
Better once than never, for never too late.

                              Exeunt.

[Scene II. Padua. Lucentio's house.]

*Enter Baptista, Vincentio, Gremio, the Pedant,
Lucentio, and Bianca, Tranio, Biondello, Grumio,
[Petruchio, Katherina, Hortensio,] and Widow;
the Servingmen with Tranio bringing in a banquet.*

Luc. At last, though long, our jarring notes agree;
And time it is, when raging war is done,
To smile at scapes and perils overblown.
My fair Bianca, bid my father welcome,

9. **banquet:** a light meal of sweets.

21. **afeard:** frightened; the widow understands the word **fears** in the sense "frightens."

25. **conceive by him:** imagine his state to be.

Banquet scene. From J. J. Boissard, *Theatrum vitae humanae* (1596).

While I with selfsame kindness welcome thine.   5
Brother Petruchio, sister Katherina,
And thou, Hortensio, with thy loving widow,
Feast with the best and welcome to my house;
My banquet is to close our stomachs up
After our great good cheer. Pray you, sit down;   10
For now we sit to chat as well as eat.

   Pet. Nothing but sit and sit, and eat and eat!

   Bap. Padua affords this kindness, son Petruchio.

   Pet. Padua affords nothing but what is kind.

   Hor. For both our sakes I would that word were   15
true.

   Pet. Now, for my life, Hortensio fears his widow.

   Wid. Then never trust me, if I be afeard.

   Pet. You are very sensible, and yet you miss my
sense: 20
I mean, Hortensio is afeard of you.

   Wid. He that is giddy thinks the world turns round.

   Pet. Roundly replied.

   Kat.   Mistress, how mean you that?

   Wid. Thus I conceive by him.   25

   Pet. Conceives by me! How likes Hortensio that?

   Hor. My widow says, thus she conceives her
tale.

   Pet. Very well mended. Kiss him for that, good
widow.   30

   Kat. "He that is giddy thinks the world turns
round":
I pray you, tell me what you meant by that.

   Wid. Your husband, being troubled with a shrew,

39. **mean:** mild; **respecting:** compared with.
45. **ha' to:** here's to.
54. **Have at you:** a challenge to be on guard.
58. **prevented:** forestalled.
61. **slipped:** released.

Measures my husband's sorrow by his woe,   35
And now you know my meaning.

  Kat. A very mean meaning.

  Wid.   Right, I mean you.

  Kat. And I am mean indeed, respecting you.

  Pet. To her, Kate!   40

  Hor. To her, widow!

  Pet. A hundred marks, my Kate does put her
down.

  Hor. That's my office.

  Pet. Spoke like an officer; ha' to thee, lad.   45
                        Drinks to Hortensio.

  Bap. How likes Gremio these quick-witted folks?

  Gre. Believe me, sir, they butt together well.

  Bia. Head and butt! An hasty-witted body
Would say your head and butt were head and horn.

  Vin. Ay, mistress bride, hath that awakened you?   50

  Bia. Ay, but not frighted me; therefore I'll sleep
again.

  Pet. Nay, that you shall not; since you have begun,
Have at you for a bitter jest or two.

  Bia. Am I your bird? I mean to shift my bush;   55
And then pursue me as you draw your bow.
You are welcome all.
        Exit Bianca [with Katherina and Widow].

  Pet. She hath prevented me. Here, Signior Tranio;
This bird you aimed at, though you hit her not:
Therefore a health to all that shot and missed.   60

  Tra. O sir! Lucentio slipped me, like his greyhound,
Which runs himself and catches for his master.

63. **something:** somewhat.
66. **deer:** pun on "dear."
68. **gird:** taunt.
70. **galled:** rubbed.
73. **good sadness:** sober earnest.
75. **assurance:** confirmation.
83. **venture:** risk; **of:** upon.
87. **A match:** the bet is agreed.

Pet. A good swift simile but something cur-
rish.

Tra. 'Tis well, sir, that you hunted for yourself;   65
'Tis thought your deer does hold you at a bay.

Bap. O ho, Petruchio! Tranio hits you now.

Luc. I thank thee for that gird, good Tranio.

Hor. Confess, confess, hath he not hit you here?

Pet. 'A has a little galled me, I confess;   70
And, as the jest did glance away from me,
'Tis ten to one it maimed you two outright.

Bap. Now, in good sadness, son Petruchio,
I think thou hast the veriest shrew of all.

Pet. Well, I say no: and therefore, for assurance,   75
Let's each one send unto his wife,
And he whose wife is most obedient
To come at first when he doth send for her
Shall win the wager which we will propose.

Hor. Content. What's the wager?   80

Luc.   Twenty crowns.

Pet. Twenty crowns!
I'll venture so much of my hawk or hound,
But twenty times so much upon my wife.

Luc. A hundred then.   85

Hor.   Content.

Pet.   A match! 'Tis done.

Hor. Who shall begin?

Luc.   That will I.
Go, Biondello, bid your mistress come to me.   90

Bio. I go.   *Exit.*

92. **be your half:** cover half your bet.

Bap. Son, I'll be your half Bianca comes.
Luc. I'll have no halves; I'll bear it all myself.

[Re-]*enter Biondello.*

How now! what news?
   Bio.   Sir, my mistress sends you word   95
That she is busy and she cannot come.
   Pet. How! She is busy and she cannot come!
Is that an answer?
   Gre.   Ay, and a kind one too;
Pray God, sir, your wife send you not a worse.   100
   Pet. I hope, better.
   Hor. Sirrah Biondello, go and entreat my wife
To come to me forthwith.   *Exit Biondello.*
   Pet.   O ho! entreat her!
Nay, then she must needs come.   105
   Hor.   I am afraid, sir,
Do what you can, yours will not be entreated.

[Re-]*enter Biondello.*

Now, where's my wife?
   Bio. She says you have some goodly jest in hand.
She will not come; she bids you come to her.   110
   Pet. Worse and worse; she will not come! O vile,
Intolerable, not to be endured!
Sirrah Grumio, go to your mistress; say
I command her come to me.   *Exit* [*Grumio*].
   Hor.   I know her answer.   115
   Pet. What?

119. **halidom:** an oath meaning "holy relics," sometimes mistaken for "holy dame," an oath on the Virgin Mary.

124. **Swinge me them:** beat them for me.

129. **awful rule:** awe-inspiring dominance.

130. **what not that's:** whatever is.

131. **fair befall thee:** may you have good fortune.

135. **as:** as though.

Hor. She will not.
Pet. The fouler fortune mine, and there an end.

Enter Katherina.

Bap. Now, by my halidom, here comes Katherina!
Kat. What is your will, sir, that you send for me? 120
Pet. Where is your sister, and Hortensio's wife?
Kat. They sit conferring by the parlor fire.
Pet. Go fetch them hither; if they deny to come,
Swinge me them soundly forth unto their husbands.
Away, I say, and bring them hither straight. 125
[*Exit Katherina.*]
Luc. Here is a wonder, if you talk of a wonder.
Hor. And so it is. I wonder what it bodes.
Pet. Marry, peace it bodes, and love, and quiet life,
An awful rule and right supremacy;
And, to be short, what not that's sweet and happy. 130
Bap. Now fair befall thee, good Petruchio!
The wager thou hast won, and I will add
Unto their losses twenty thousand crowns,
Another dowry to another daughter,
For she is changed, as she had never been. 135
Pet. Nay, I will win my wager better yet
And show more sign of her obedience,
Her new-built virtue and obedience.

Enter Kate, Bianca, and Widow.

See where she comes and brings your froward wives
As prisoners to her womanly persuasion. 140

145. **duty:** obedience.
149. **laying:** wagering.
162. **Confounds:** destroys; **fame:** reputation.
163. **meet:** suitable; **amiable:** lovable.
164. **moved:** angry; vexed.
165. **ill-seeming:** unseemly.

Katherine, that cap of yours becomes you not:
Off with that bauble, throw it underfoot.

  Wid. Lord! let me never have a cause to sigh
Till I be brought to such a silly pass!

  Bia. Fie! what a foolish duty call you this?   145

  Luc. I would your duty were as foolish too;
The wisdom of your duty, fair Bianca,
Hath cost me five hundred crowns since suppertime.

  Bia. The more fool you for laying on my duty.

  Pet. Katherine, I charge thee, tell these headstrong 150
    women
What duty they do owe their lords and husbands.

  Wid. Come, come, you're mocking; we will have no
    telling.

  Pet. Come on, I say; and first begin with her.   155

  Wid. She shall not.

  Pet. I say she shall: and first begin with her.

  Kat. Fie, fie! unknit that threat'ning unkind brow,
And dart not scornful glances from those eyes
To wound thy lord, thy king, thy governor.   160
It blots thy beauty as frosts do bite the meads,
Confounds thy fame as whirlwinds shake fair buds,
And in no sense is meet or amiable.
A woman moved is like a fountain troubled,
Muddy, ill-seeming, thick, bereft of beauty;   165
And while it is so, none so dry or thirsty
Will deign to sip or touch one drop of it.
Thy husband is thy lord, thy life, thy keeper,
Thy head, thy sovereign; one that cares for thee,
And for thy maintenance commits his body   170

182. **graceless:** wicked.

192. **big:** defiant.

193. **heart:** spirit; courage.

198. **vail your stomachs:** diminish your arrogance; **no boot:** useless.

To painful labor both by sea and land,
To watch the night in storms, the day in cold,
Whilst thou liest warm at home, secure and safe;
And craves no other tribute at thy hands
But love, fair looks, and true obedience;   175
Too little payment for so great a debt.
Such duty as the subject owes the prince,
Even such a woman oweth to her husband;
And when she is froward, peevish, sullen, sour,
And not obedient to his honest will,   180
What is she but a foul contending rebel
And graceless traitor to her loving lord?
I am ashamed that women are so simple
To offer war where they should kneel for peace,
Or seek for rule, supremacy, and sway,   185
When they are bound to serve, love, and obey.
Why are our bodies soft and weak and smooth,
Unapt to toil and trouble in the world,
But that our soft conditions and our hearts
Should well agree with our external parts?   190
Come, come, you forward and unable worms!
My mind hath been as big as one of yours,
My heart as great, my reason haply more,
To bandy word for word and frown for frown;
But now I see our lances are but straws,   195
Our strength as weak, our weakness past compare,
That seeming to be most which we indeed least are.
Then vail your stomachs, for it is no boot,
And place your hands below your husband's foot:
In token of which duty, if he please,   200

205. **toward:** tractable.
208. **sped:** done for.
210. **the white:** (1) Bianca ("white" in Italian), (2) the bull's-eye.

My hand is ready; may it do him ease.

   Pet. Why, there's a wench! Come on and kiss me, Kate.

   Luc. Well, go thy ways, old lad, for thou shalt ha't.

   Vin. 'Tis a good hearing when children are toward. 205

   Luc. But a harsh hearing when women are froward.

   Pet. Come, Kate, we'll to bed.

We three are married, but you two are sped.

'Twas I won the wager, [*To Lucentio*] though you hit the white; 210

And, being a winner, God give you good night!

                 Exit Petruchio [*with Katherina*].

   Hor. Now, go thy ways; thou hast tamed a curst shrew.

   Luc. 'Tis a wonder, by your leave, she will be tamed so. 215

                      [*Exeunt.*]

KEY TO
Famous Lines

No profit grows where is no pleasure ta'en;
In brief, sir, study what you most affect.   [*Tranio*—I. i. 39-40]

I come to wive it wealthy in Padua;
If wealthily, then happily in Padua.   [*Petruchio*—I. ii. 76-77]

Nothing comes amiss so money comes withal.
[*Grumio*—I. ii. 82-83]

Old fashions please me best.   [*Bianca*—III. i. 86]

Who wooed in haste and means to wed at leisure.
[*Katherina*—III. ii. 13]

This is a way to kill a wife with kindness.
[*Petruchio*—IV. i. 206]

Our purses shall be proud, our garments poor,
For 'tis the mind that makes the body rich.
[*Petruchio*—IV. iii. 179-80]